A HISTORY OF ISRAEL

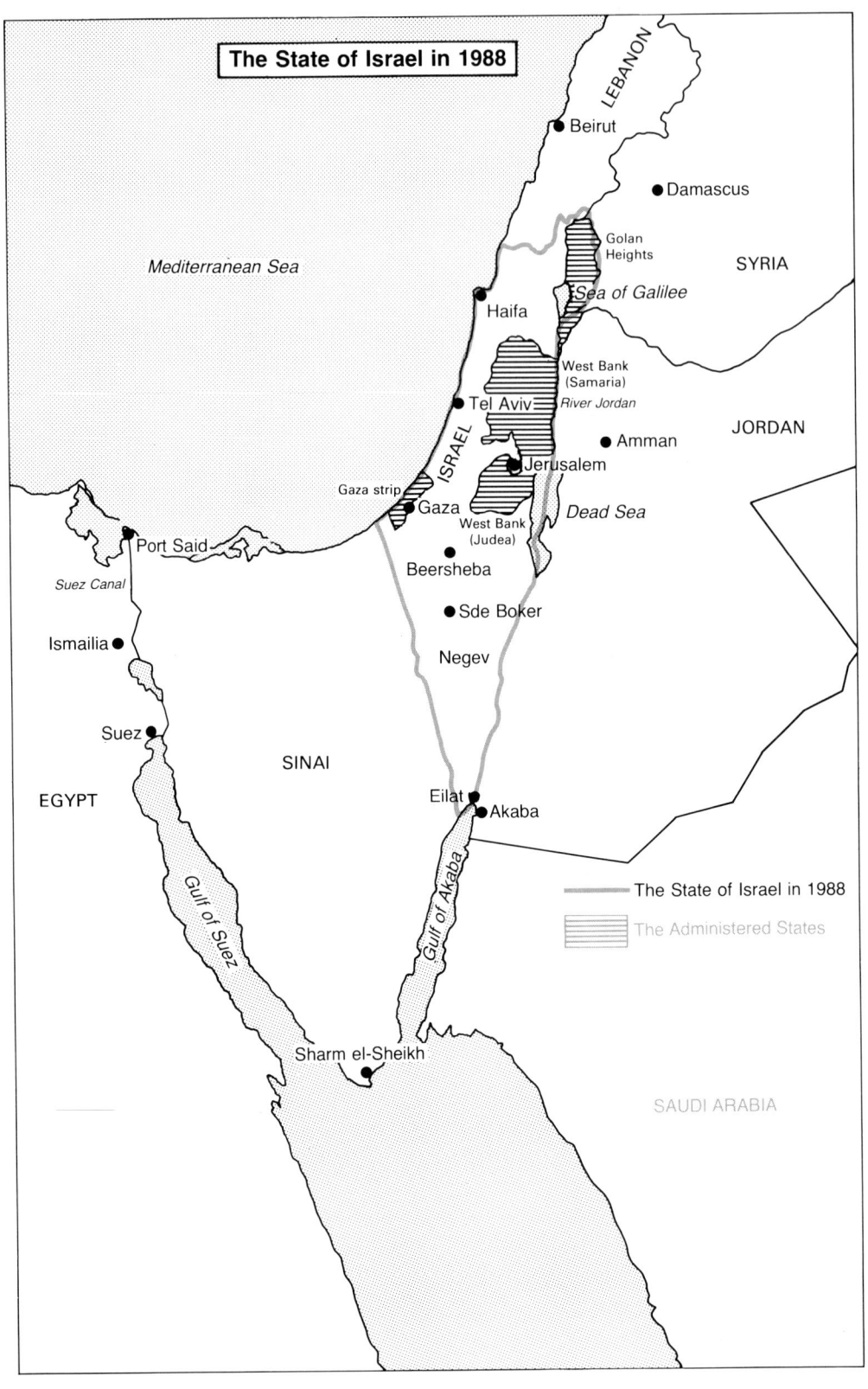

A HISTORY OF
ISRAEL

*The birth, growth and development
of today's Jewish State*

RINNA SAMUEL

Weidenfeld and Nicolson   *London*

*This overview of the long history of their country
is most affectionately dedicated to Tali, Yoram, Naomi,
Shani and Carmel*

Copyright © Rinna Samuel 1989

First published in Great Britain by
George Weidenfeld & Nicolson Limited
91 Clapham High Street, London SW4 7TA

Picture Researcher: Patricia Mandel

All rights reserved. No part of this publication
may be reproduced, stored in a retrieval
system, or transmitted in any form or by any
means, electronic, mechanical, photocopying,
recording or otherwise, without the prior
permission of the copyright owner.

ISBN 0 297 79329 2

Printed by Butler & Tanner Ltd,
Frome and London

Contents

Illustration Acknowledgments
vii

1 *In the Beginning*
1

2 *Dispersions*
18

3 *From Balfour to Ben-Gurion*
35

4 *The Jewish State*
55

5 *The Cost of Independence*
73

6 *The First Decade*
93

7 *Confrontation and Achievement*
109

8 *The Noose Tightens: Terrorism, War and Victory*
129

9 *Begin, Sadat and the Peace Treaty*
147

10 *Israel at Forty*
164

Index
179

Illustration Acknowledgments

The author and publishers would like to thank the following for kind permission to reproduce the photographs in the book: David Harris, 1, 56, 57; Bildarchiv Foto Marburg, 2; J. Allan Cash, 3; Photo IZIS, 4, 46, 66; Gemma Levine, 5; Mandel Archive, 6, 9, 10, 14, 16, 37, 47, 68; Leiden University Library, 7; Weidenfeld Archives, 8, 51, 61, 82; Foto Mas, 11; Alfred Rubens, 12; Israel Labour Archives, 13; Central Zionist Archives, 15, 18, 22, 23, 26; BBC Hulton Picture Library, 17, 24, 25, 58; Haganah Archives, 19, 28, 29, 33; Imperial War Museum, 20, 32, 35; Jewish Agency, Jerusalem, 21, 30; IPPA, 31; Associated Press, 27, 38, 39, 62, 69, 70, 80, 95, 96; Britain/Israel Public Affairs Committee (BIPAC), 34, 36, 40, 42, 43, 44, 49, 52, 65, 67, 78, 86, 87, 88, 89, 91; The Kressel Library, Yarnton, 41; Keystone Press, 45, 83; Israel Government Press Office, 48, 75, 76, 81, 90; W. Braun, 50; United Nations Department of Public Information, 53; Nancy Durrell McKenna, 54, 94, 99; Rex Features, 55, 84, 93, 98; David Rubinger, 59; John Hillelson, 60 (photo: Burt Glinn), 71 and 73 (photos: Cornell Capa), 74 (photo: Micha Bar-Am), 85 (photo: Robert Capa); International Labour Office, 63; Ronald Sheridan's Photo-Library, 64; Photo Ross, 72; Popperfoto, 77, 92, 97; Mike Busselle, 79; Weizmann Institute Foundation, 100.
(Picture research by Patricia Mandel.)

CHAPTER 1

In the Beginning

Because Israel is, at one and the same time, the name of a modern and sovereign state now entering its fifth decade, of a people, the Jews, who have believed for thousands of years that they inhabit this land as of historic right, and of a faith that, to varying degrees but always to some extent, connects one Jew to another, even the most compact, the most diligently pruned history of Israel must deal with context as well as with content, with past as well as present. Of course, the past lives on in us all, buried, as a rule, in the protective unconscious, operating in hidden ways. But, within most Israelis, it functions actively, openly; part of a collective consciousness that influences everyday life, shaping the national self-image and colouring a shared sense of what the future may hold. The past then, or at least some of its components, must be glanced at before contemporary Israel can be properly touched upon, let alone understood.

Thus, although it took place some thirty-five centuries ago, the Old Testament story of Abraham, of the charge laid upon him by God, and of the binding promise ('Unto thy seed will I give this land') that accompanied it, is where, however incongruous it may seem, the annals of the modern State of Israel must begin. Not with the Proclamation of Independence in 1948, not with any subsequent event in the state's history, however crucial or dramatic, but with the biblical account of Abraham and what happened to this simple, semi-nomadic, no longer young herdsman, living with his large family in Mesopotamia (today's Iraq) in a place called Ur.

We are given some facts about him: we learn from his family tree that he is descended from Noah's son Shem; we are informed (the Bible, however terse, rarely omits illuminating nuances) that he is in no sense either particularly attractive or noble. And, early on (*Genesis* 12:2), we are also told that God, whose ways are indeed mysterious, chose to call upon this entirely ordinary man to leave his homeland and set out for an unknown place to fulfil an ultimately unclear purpose. It is perhaps no less remarkable that Abraham instantly obeyed; he gathered up his extended family and chattels, set off for and eventually reached the Land of Canaan — much later to be known as Palestine — thus becoming the first of the three Patriarchs and the founder of the Jewish nation.

'Unto thy seed will I give this land' was the pledge. It was renewed often in the course of Abraham's long lifetime; the wording was not always identical but the message never changed, becoming increasingly specific until it acquired the tone, terminology and precision of a formal deed or covenant: 'Unto thy seed have I given this land, from the River of Egypt unto the great river, the river Euphrates.' When Abraham was nearly a hundred years old, God appeared to him and repeated the promise: 'I will give unto thee, and to thy seed after thee ... all the land of Canaan for an ever-lasting possession.'

The subsequent relationship between Abraham and the Lord, the continuing, difficult demands made on Abraham, the often agonizing tests to which he is put, are, in themselves, not immediately relevant. Nor is it important to establish whether Abraham really lived or rather was an extremely useful symbol. What does matter, what directly and critically affects daily life not only in Israel but throughout the Middle East and therefore much of today's world — constituting for millions of men and women either inspiration and holy writ or anachronism, legend and what is now called 'disinformation' — is the Promise and the many possible implications and interpretations fastened on to it in the course of millennia.

The Hebrews (as those early Jews were known) did not prosper in their new land; drought, famine and bad luck dogged them. When Abraham's grandson, Jacob, was old enough, he led the family (some seventy people in all) out of Canaan and down to Egypt, where conditions reputedly were better. This, too, was a bold and effective act for which Jacob — best known these days for the life and times of his favourite son, the brightly coated Joseph — has perhaps not received adequate credit.

The Hebrews stayed in Egypt for hundreds of years, multiplying mightily. Fecundity, however, was their only, if somewhat mixed, blessing. For most of their stay there, they lived as slaves, wretchedly engaged in forced labour and finally threatened with what amounted to genocide. Deliverance came *circa* 1266 BC, in the form of a liberation movement led by Moses, a Jew brought up from infancy in the Pharaonic household and destined to become a

1 In biblical Shechem, site of modern Nablus, Abraham built an altar to the Lord, Joseph's remains were buried and Joshua made a covenant with the Children of Israel.

2 Moses holding high the Ten Commandments – as Rembrandt, in seventeenth-century Holland, imagined him and the Tablets to be.

political, military and spiritual leader of unusual, possibly unique, dimensions, endowed with penetrating intelligence and superb administrative ability. Larger than life, he comes down through time as a monumental figure, bidden by God to save His entrapped people. Moses brought the Children of Israel out of captivity across the dividing Red Sea, into the desert and back to the frontiers of Canaan, a journey which lasted for forty years and is still commemorated by Jews the world over as the first day of Passover, an abiding symbol of the flight to freedom. The Exodus from Egypt, however, was more than the Long March of the ancient Jews, more than a deeply motivated return to a never-forgotten homeland. It was in the desert, during those four arid decades, that God gave to Moses the Ten Commandments; these injunctions have served ever since as central themes of the laws by which the Western world tries, for the most part in vain, to live. Along with them, Moses also received the Law (the Torah in Hebrew), the meticulously detailed codex (contained in the first five books of the Bible) by which Jews are ordered to live and which is still, for those who are observant (and therefore, in many ways, for much of the population of the State of Israel), not only a viable guide to daily conduct, but also applicable, if properly understood, to all times and all situations, and in its essence immutable.

Nothing less than his amazing ability to put the fear of God into them could have enabled Moses to keep the twelve Tribes (according to tradition the descendants of Jacob and known collectively as the Israelites) – protesting, complaining, filled with doubt and on the verge of mutiny – wandering around the sun-scorched massif of southern Sinai. But that ability was his – and ruthlessly he kept them there, waiting until a new generation would mature, one born in the wildernesss, knowing nothing of the corrosion of slavery. Somewhere between the twelfth and eleventh centuries BC, skilfully directed by Moses' young lieutenant Joshua, the Tribes crossed over the River Jordan, fording it north of the Dead Sea; the ensuing campaigns, which resulted in the conquest of most of Canaan, lasted about seven years. Moses was not with the Children of Israel; he died within sight of the Land, never entering it: 'I have let you see it with your eyes,' said the Lord, 'but you shall not go over there' (*Deuteronomy* 34:4).

Although the Israelites took the plains and central hill country, the coastal villages and mountain areas stubbornly remained under control of a bevy of tribal kings: Canaanites, Amorites, Edomites, Moabites, and later the Philistines (whose presence lingers in the name 'Palestine'). All the smite-ing and smote-ing – of which there is so much in the Bible – did not suffice to

3 Jericho, south-east of Jerusalem, possibly the oldest city in the world, was already a walled town with a long history when Joshua's forces arrived.

4 Solomon's Pillars, and the smelting pits from which his slaves extracted copper ore, are just north of Eilat, from where the King himself set out for Ophir and Tarshish.

secure the whole country for Joshua's forces. Jericho, of course, fell to the sound of rams' horns; the sun and the moon obediently stood still at Gibeon; but the 'exceedingly good land ... which flows with milk and honey' had to be partly shared, at least for the time being. Even what belonged to the Tribes had to be divided up amongst them: two of the Tribes (and half of a third) stayed east of the Jordan; the remaining nine and a half bickered and bargained for some three centuries about the justice and/or injustice of Joshua's decisions in this regard, mostly deployed against each other but always as one when assaulted from outside.

In the vivid procession of seers, statesmen and soldiers that winds through the history of Israel, it is likely that the single, most creative personality was King David, the good-looking, gifted son of a Bethlehem farmer, who won his laurels when, a page at the court of King Saul (the first anointed King of Israel), and armed only with a slingshot, he trounced the Philistine Goliath. Not surprisingly, David went on to better, if not bigger, things. He married Saul's daughter; he endeared himself to Saul's beloved son Jonathan; he was victorious over the rest of the Philistines, thus expanding the limits of the Kingdom of Israel, and was then anointed its sole ruler. In an astonishingly crowded, success-crowned and frequently wicked life, he found time also to acquire the City of Jerusalem and to make it his capital; to write most, if not all, of the Psalms; and to play the harp surpassingly well. Understandably, there is more in the Bible about David than about any other king, and it seems natural, therefore, that in the Israel of the 1980s the local 'Oscar' bears his still luminous name.

It was left to David's son, the sage and highly uxorious Solomon (*circa* 950 BC), to put up the Temple in Jerusalem which housed the Jewish Holy of Holies. 'Wiser than all other men' (1 *Kings* 4:31), he too was blessed with an abundance of talents. He was the composer of all 3,000 Proverbs and the author of the beautiful *Song of Songs*; he was also a shrewd economic planner, an unconventional and imaginative diplomat, and a master builder. Working with copper, stone, gold and cedar wood atop Jerusalem's Mount Moriah (known today as the Temple Mount), he designed the edifice that was to become a focal point, not to say an emblem, of national unity. Long after Solomon's Temple was destroyed, its memory glowed in the heart of Jews, wherever they were.

The feuding between the Tribes appeared endemic, a divisiveness which heightened after Solomon's death, fatally weakening the easy-going, greedy, Torah-evading tenth-century BC kingdoms – of which there were now two: Judea (from which the word Jew originates) in the south and Israel in the north. Moral slackness and corruption would bring catastrophe, thundered the Prophets, men like Hosea, Amos, Isaiah, Jeremiah and Ezekiel whose very names – even today – bespeak rebuke and retribution. Sneered at, often menaced, representing nothing and no one but what they themselves perceived as the one God and His truth, they held forth on unpopular issues such as social justice, care for the needy, righteousness and honesty. In the end, the predicted calamities befell both kingdoms: Israel was overrun by the Assyrians in 722 BC and Judea was invaded by Babylon's Nebuchadnezzar in 586 BC, the Temple destroyed and the Jews led into Babylonian captivity. 'If I forget thee O Jerusalem, let my right hand lose its cunning' sang the Jews sadly by the waters of Babylon, holding tight to the hope that Ezekiel's prophecy of dead bones revived was also a blueprint of their immediate future.

The dispersion of the Jews had left some in Judea, though Jerusalem itself was laid waste; others escaped to Egypt; most settled in Babylon, itself to be conquered in 539 BC by Cyrus of Persia. The pendulum of history, which swings with such violence in the Middle East, moved again, reversing fortunes and redirecting events. Where Nebuchadnezzar had violated and scattered, Cyrus restored and resettled. He not only ordered the return of the Jews to their ancestral homeland, but also that Solomon's Temple be rebuilt. About 520 BC the massive 'renovation' began; within five years, the Second Temple was dedicated, destined to stand for another 588 years. Led by one of David's descendants, and constituting a first wave of immigration, 42,000 Jews returned almost at once to establish the Second Jewish Commonwealth, with another wave following in 450 BC.

Viewed from the perspective of the gorgeous palaces of ancient Persia, the movements, arrangements and subsequent squabbles of the people of Judea were not of great interest. Judea was only one of several small, distant states, ruled by Persian governors (one of the first, Nehemiah, like the first British High Commissioner to Palestine in 1920, was a Jew) and permitted in the main to run itself so long as the Jews were punctual about paying their heavy taxes.

The pendulum moved again, sharply; the trekking of the great powers across the Land went on; Persian rule ended when Alexander the Great appeared. In 332 BC, Judea became a Greek province, but when Alexander died, his

5 Cradle of Christianity, one of Islam's holiest cities, at the very heart of Judaism and Israel's capital, Jerusalem has retained intact throughout the centuries her beauty, complexity and remarkable aura.

6 A reconstruction of the inner courtyard of the Second Temple.

empire fell apart and, in the bloody internal wars fought by his successors, Judea changed hands with dizzying rapidity. By the time the dust settled, in 210 BC, the Land had been ceded to Hellenist Syria and the scene set for a notable drama of repression and resistance.

The reigning Syrian King, Antiochus IV Epiphanes, was irritated by the Jews, by their separatist behaviour, their strange monotheistic creed and practices. It was high time they lived well-rounded Hellenistic lives, controlled, and adorned, by gods and goddesses like everyone else in the vicinity. But the Jews were not known as a stiff-necked people for nothing. When Antiochus demanded an end to the observance of the Sabbath, to circumcision (though he knew that this expressed Abraham's covenant with God) and to abstention from swine flesh, he provoked what may have been the first war ever fought for freedom of worship and conscience. Some Jews were prepared to accept the status quo, but when the Temple was polluted, dedicated to the Olympian Zeus (a.k.a. Jupiter) and the abominated swine sacrificed within its precincts, few could deny either the reality or the meaning of these events. The revolt, led by a middle-aged priest, Matityahu of the Hasmonean family (who lived in the Judean townlet of Modi'in with his five sons, the Maccabees), began when Antiochus' officers swaggered into Modi'in to ensure correct worship of the Greek gods. The Maccabees were ready for them; shouting 'For Torah and Covenant', Matityahu spearheaded the attack and took the soldiers completely by surprise. Though raggle-taggle and barely trained, the Jewish rebels epitomized a citizen's army, brave, resourceful and, above all, strongly motivated.

A familiar tale? Maybe, but as edifying in 164 BC as it has proved since. The achievements, to say nothing of the skill, of the Maccabees seemed limitless: Jerusalem was retaken; the Temple purified; and the borders of the Land stretched till those achieved by Solomon were reattained. However, times, it appeared, were not propitious for expansion; enthusiasm, togetherness and *esprit de corps* gradually faded, to be replaced by intense hostilities on matters concerning religious belief and behaviour. Judea was torn in two: the Pharisees interpreted the Torah broadly, minimizing the exclusive position of the Temple, arguing that knowledge was not the prerogative of the priesthood; the Sadducees, basically an 'establishment' party, made it clear that they considered their opponents to be dangerous revolutionaries. Given a situation closely resembling civil war, it was on the cards that the Romans, having assessed the Land's great strategic value (as did the Assyrians, the Babylonians and the Greeks before them), should also try *their* luck. What

7 A tenth-century *Book of the Maccabees* shows Matityahu slaying a man about to sacrifice a pig at Modi'in. Each Hannukah holiday (commemorating the Maccabees), Israeli children relay a flaming torch from Modi'in to Jerusalem.

better timing than when the Jews were busy battling against each other, Syria having only recently been swallowed up by the Roman Empire?

The Romans set up a puppet kingdom in Judea, putting their men in charge. A governor was not enough; a *bona fide* puppet state called for a puppet king. This dubious role was assigned to Herod the Great, during whose reign Jesus was born in Bethlehem, lived and preached in Galilee and Jerusalem until around 30 AD, when the Romans ordered him to be crucified in Jerusalem. Behind him, Jesus left a handful of devoted followers; it was they who were to found Christianity, the second major international religion to be cradled in the Land. In twentieth-century Israel, Herod's name is associated primarily with the virtually impregnable fortress he built for himself on the huge flat rock of Masada, in the heart of the Judean desert, and also with one of the Temple walls which he erected (it still stands): the western wall, better known as the Wailing Wall.

Around 4 AD Judea became a sub-province ruled by a procurator answerable to the Roman proconsul in Syria. The Jews were not the only people crushed by Imperial Rome, but no other nation paid so heavy a price for the loss of statehood. Those who accepted the *Pax Romana* stayed pretty much where and as they were, but the Jews were unable either to abandon their Law or to lose their identity as the Chosen People in the melting-pot of the Roman–Hellenistic civilization. The death throes of the Jewish Commonwealth took the form of guerrilla uprisings against the Romans, culminating in the War of the Jews against Rome (66–70/73 AD), which, according to Roman records, was one of the fiercest struggles ever fought by the proud Legions. It took three more years of bitter fighting for Jewish resistance to be overcome, for Jerusalem to be razed again and for the Second Temple to be gutted. One pocket of blatant defiance remained: on Herod's Masada, 1,500 feet above the level of the Dead Sea, nearly a thousand Jewish men, women and children who had survived the fall of Jerusalem still refused to surrender to Rome. For months, they held out against repeated Roman attempts to dislodge them. In 73 AD, when the Romans broke through, it was discovered that the besieged Jews had killed themselves rather than give in.

However, the urge for independence, self-government and self-expression was overwhelming. Sixty years after the Temple was reduced to ashes, the Jews rose up again, led this time by Simeon Bar-Kosiba (nicknamed Bar-Kochba or 'Son of a Star'), and engaged the Romans for several years. Sixty thousand Jews perished in that desperate stand, but in 135 AD the

8 Herod cut vast cisterns, storerooms and palaces into the steep walls of the cliff on which Masada was built. Amenities included gardens, mosaic floors and a swimming-pool.

Romans at last snuffed out the revolt; punishment was swift, savage and liberally meted out. Jerusalem was obliterated from the map; the name *Aelia Capitolina* and a temple to Jupiter were substituted; thousands of Jews were sold into slavery and all Jews banished in perpetuity from their former capital — though, for centuries to come, small Jewish communities existed elsewhere in the country.

The lost Land remained central to both the theory and the practice of Jewish law. Wherever they were, Jews turned in prayer, as they turn today, to Jerusalem; the days of fasting and mourning marked on the Jewish calendar, which they took with them into exile, are nearly all commemorations of the ancient sorrows; the prayers for rain and dew were chanted in seasons when the soil of the Land (however far away) required these, and the words 'Next year in Jerusalem', annually repeated by Jews throughout the world, lost none of their force or meaning.

The Middle Eastern merry-go-round went on revolving. The spread and, by the beginning of the fourth century, the official status of Christianity within the Roman Empire kept the Land in the public eye. Within a century, Christian pilgrims flooded the country; churches sprang up everywhere, as did monasteries: the first, deep in Judea, was founded in 428 AD. An influx of devout newcomers from Western Europe quickly improved the status and well-being of the local brethren; when aristocratic matrons, a real empress among them, arived to live out their golden years in the sanctity of Jerusalem and Bethlehem, they generated the construction of even more churches, hospices and cloisters. In fact, the Land was now the core of Christendom, piety and penitence combining neatly to create prosperity. Not that tranquillity reigned; far from it. Throughout the fourth and fifth centuries, instead of Jewish internecine tension, Christian theological feuds tore at the fabric of the still-infant religion. Weakened from within, preyed on by fanatics, undergoing agonizing reappraisals of its very nature, in 614 AD, when the Persians captured Jerusalem from the Romans, Christian dominion in the Land entered a terminal phase. For fifteen years, Persian luck held; Syria, Egypt and the Holy Land were taken and the gates of Constantinople, political and administrative kernel of Byzantium, reached. But the blood-letting was costlier than either side had envisaged, and a third party made its appearance. Younger, hungrier, more extremist than either Rome or Persia, far more single-mindedly bent on victory, the Moslems entered the picture and stayed there, at the forefront, for what, by any standards, was a long time.

In the Beginning

The Moslem conquest of the Near and Middle East, North Africa and Spain — turning-points in history — followed in the wake of the death of Mohammed, a man who, like Abraham, was seemingly totally commonplace. A camel driver, one of the many who led merchant caravans in and to Syria and the Holy Land (which, from here on and for a while, will be referred to as Palestine), he had picked up from the Jewish and Christian traders, whose cargoes he ferried across the sand, nothing less than the message of monotheism. He had taken it back to Mecca with him, plus a formulation so simple that any Bedouin could understand it: God is one; Mohammed is his Prophet. Islam spread like wildfire. For the next thousand years, the Islamic Empire was to include much of Asia, Africa and Southern Europe. By 636 AD, both Damascus (capital of Syria) and Jerusalem belonged to a new master. Naming it for Omar (who conquered Jerusalem), the Moslems built a magnificent mosque (the Dome of the Rock) on the site on which the Temple once stood, and from which they believed Mohammed had ascended to Heaven — a belief which made the Land sacred also to Islam. At first, Moslem rule in the Land was tolerant; Mohammed had adopted many Jewish principles and fostered friendly ties with the Jews. Jewish settlement in Jerusalem was renewed and the Jews appointed guardians of the Temple Mount in return for their aid to the Moslem army. But with the transfer of the Moslem political capital from Damascus (which was controlled by one Moslem dynasty) to Baghdad (controlled by another), the position of Jews and Christians alike worsened and, when power passed to the Egyptian Fatimid dynasty (which in 973 AD founded Cairo), taxation reached a new high and persecution a new low.

Palestine had been ruled by the Moslems for nearly 400 years when an order came, in 1009 AD, from the Fatimid caliph demanding that the Church of the Holy Sepulchre in Jerusalem be destroyed. The order was never fully executed, but world Christianity was outraged. Hakim's decree set off an anti-Moslem chain reaction of fury which, in turn, ignited the tragic and protracted sequence of the Christian Holy Wars, the Crusades, in Palestine, of which the first was launched in 1096 AD, the last nearly 200 years later. Jerusalem — taken by 12,000 exhausted, if elated, European nobles, knights, serfs and freemen — became the jewel in the crown of the Crusader Latin kingdom (known also as Outremer or the land beyond the sea), formed on the feudal patern of medieval Europe and entirely dependent on it; the Holy Sepulchre was restored; Omar's mosque was converted for Christian use; and Crusader castles, churches, manor houses and hospices were built throughout Palestine — their weatherbeaten remnants still to be seen. Predictably enough,

9 Saladin's Saracen army, with Jerusalem's Mosque of Omar (the Dome of the Rock, built between 687 and 691 AD) in the background.

10 From a fourteenth-century French history, the Crusader attack (1099 AD) on Jerusalem: the armies of Godfrey de Bouillon that captured the city confront those of Saladin, who took it back in 1187.

poor organization, inadequate preparation, the daunting distance from their European bases and greater Moslem vigour, even perhaps competence, in due course brought about a succession of Crusader defeats — the most spectacular being the victory of the Saracen warrior Saladin on a plain between Tiberias and Nazareth in 1187 AD, which returned Jerusalem to the Moslems. Jerusalem changed hands again, not for the last time. In 1258 AD, Saladin's successors, the Egyptian Mamelukes, took over; these were mercenary soldiers, former slaves, mostly of Georgian and Circassian origin, who set up their headquarters elsewhere in the country, running it, to the extent that it was run at all, until 1516 AD, when the Turks turned up for their undistinguished, negligent 400-year-long innings, the most indifferent regime that the Land had yet known.

CHAPTER 2

Dispersions

The curtain never came down on Jewish life in the Land; despite the laxity, cruelty and greed of their Ottoman overlords, small Jewish communities, unprotected and impoverished, maintained centres of intensive biblical study and prayer, mostly in Jerusalem, Safed, Tiberias and Hebron, modestly supported by donations from abroad, their existence unsweetened by much milk or honey. 'In their land,' wrote a seventeenth-century traveller, 'the Jews live as strangers, open to all oppression and deprivation.' Beyond administrative suppression and attack by Moslem fanatics, there were other trials to be borne: drought, epidemic, locust and a shrinking population which meant no trade or industry. In short, decline. Little wonder then that in the eighteenth century Napoleon Bonaparte, having conquered Egypt, felt sure that he could scoop up the rest of the Turkish Empire with almost no effort at all. In fact, most of Palestine was already in his hands in 1799 when the Turks, aided by the British navy, made an unexpected stand at Acre, forcing Napoleon to withdraw. From then on, however, European influence in Palestine grew, mainly via the special privileges (called 'capitulations') given to European citizens, to European guardianship of churches and church property, and to the frequent visits of European 'royals' to the Holy Land. The isolation was ending; the time growing ripe for a development which, to an unimaginable extent, would alter the future of the Land and of those who claimed it as of right. The new factor, the Zionist movement, was also of European origin.

There were places, and times, in the many lands and centuries of their dispersion that the Jews were permitted limited power and relatively untrammelled creativity as doctors, astronomers, philosophers and poets; sometimes they even became sought-after advisers. This was true of the Golden Age of Spain under Moslem rule. Jews had lived in Iberia from just before, or just after, the destruction of the Second Temple and, in medieval times, played more or less leading roles in cultural and economic life. The best known of these distinguished Spanish Jews was the great twelfth-century scholar and physician Moses Maimonides (the Rambam), though even he — who had served as personal physician to the great Saladin — was confronted by persecution in his native Cordova and chose to make his permanent home in Egypt. But as Christianity claimed the dominant position, the situation of the Jews worsened; the 'Jewish question' began to perturb the Church, and the demand that arose for the mass conversion of Spanish Jewry eventually found expression in the ruthless anti-Jewish massacres of 1391, which led, in turn, to the notorious Inquisition and, in 1492, to the ultimatum: conversion or expulsion. By then, the Jews had been forced to wear special badges and over 60,000 had been killed; that year, 160,000 Jews left Spain and 20,000 more perished in the search for a new life; 50,000 were baptized, stayed in Spain and continued, but always secretly, to live as Jews. The sense of outrage and betrayal that gripped Spanish Jewry was deep and lasted a long time. For several hundred years, no Jews lived in Spain and few visited it; the first synagogue following the Expulsion was not opened until 1967, and it was only in 1986 that Israel and Spain exchanged ambassadors.

Each country dealt with its Jews differently and with different results. In medieval France, Society, most professions and all government jobs were hermetically closed to Jews, upon whom unspeakable horrors were visited by the Crusaders *en route* to the Holy Land; four times between 1182 and 1321, the Jews were expelled from France and recalled, and for nearly half a century no Jews were there at all. In Germany, there was also a constant process of local in-and-out, but no general expulsion. In England, on the other hand, small groups were encouraged to settle and to participate in the monarchy's financial well-being — for which they were despised by the masses. In the thirteenth century, they were expelled, fleeing mostly to France and Flanders, and their property confiscated; they were not to return until 300 years later (still without civil rights). Step by step, little by little, they began to achieve political emancipation, the privilege of attending university and permission to enter the free professions. The scale of discrimination and brutality was most horrifying, however, in Eastern Europe — Poland, Russia, Lithuania — where anti-Jewish pogroms and the devastation of Jewish communities were standard procedure, rendered easier for the authorities by the invention of the Pale of Settlement.

11 A fifteenth-century carving in Barcelona Cathedral shows Spanish Jews with distinguishing circles on their hoods, as ordered by church edict in 1215.

12 Right: From a nineteenth-century drawing: a Lithuanian Jew, his wife and daughter.

Established in the eighteenth century, the Pale was a huge area stretching from the Baltic Sea to the Black Sea in which Jews (eventually some four million) were made to live, restricted in their occupations, forbidden to farm and subject to unending harshness, indignity and grinding poverty. In a country in which all who were not noble or affluent lived marginal and brutalized lives, the Jews, driven into the Pale like cattle, were the natural victims of drunken and violent peasant mobs. Twentieth-century art, literature and cinema have romanticized life in the *shtetl*, the crowded unlovely ramshackle Jewish townlet of the Pale, but the reality, of course, was otherwise.

The pattern held elsewhere too. Perhaps the oldest of the diasporas was Arabia: Jews had lived in Yemen since the sixth century BC. Mohammed had hoped to convert them to Islam; his hopes dashed, he demanded that they be taxed for the right to live among Moslems. As wards of the government known as 'people of the protection', they were sheltered, debased and separated from everyone else, allowed to worship in their own way, but forbidden to wear bright clothing, bear arms, use saddles or engage in the same work as Moslems; and all orphaned Jewish babies were instantly converted.

Although locked in ghettos, confined to special streets and sections of towns and cities, relegated to the status of non-citizens of the countries in which they lived, and, for the most part, threadbare and undernourished, the Jews continued to derive spiritual and emotional sustenance from the splendour of the Bible, from the never-fading challenge of interpreting it, from the yearly round of Jewish Holy days, and from the peace and inner beauty of the weekly Sabbath. To survive as Jews, they created various forms of autonomy, rigorously carrying out religious rules and injunctions, operating their own systems of social welfare and education, and developing languages for their exile. Hebrew was sacred, reserved entirely for prayer and exegesis, so secular alternatives had to be found: in Central and Eastern Europe, Yiddish was born, combining German with Hebrew; and in the countries along the Mediterranean, Jews developed Ladino, basing it on medieval Spanish and Hebrew.

Then came emancipation; gradually, again in different ways at different times and in different places. It had taken close to 2,000 years to come, but equality, in varying degrees, at last arrived; first in France with the Revolution which proclaimed 'Liberty, Equality, Fraternity' and which saw fit to include the Jews among its beneficiaries. It moved to Belgium; knocked over the ghetto walls of Italy; put finishing touches on the integration of Jews into

British society; and, by 1871, in effect, had provided civil rights to the Jews of Western Europe, including Germany and Spain, which had no Jews but, in 1868, withdrew its original order of expulsion. Western emancipation however did not lessen, except very briefly, the inhumanity of the Tsarist regime in Russia, nor did the so-called Jewish problem vanish permanently as might have been expected. Still, there was dazzling new freedom in an unfamiliar world; the Jews of the West, incarcerated for so long, feasted their eyes on the visual glories of Europe, rushed to listen to the music they had not heard before and to read about the exciting new ideas of classlessness and the betterment of man's lot on earth – political credos that held particular relevance for them, and readied themselves to participate in the stimulating, fascinating, seductive ways of life suddenly revealed.

For this equality, for these golden opportunities, for this enlightenment, surely the habits of exclusion could be abandoned – or, at least, modernized: German, French and English allowed to displace Yiddish; synagogue to be attended less often; the distinctive, enforced and binding constraints of the past loosened or done away with? Many European Jews yearned for the release – and found it; others were not allowed to try it; and some, out-of-hand, rejected the alien allure and went on waiting for the Messiah to deliver His people. But roughly at this juncture, two major forces began to converge in Jewish life: one that was forming within the dark victimized Pale; the other quickening inside the bright centre of the emanicipation itself; both dedicated not to denial or acceptance of a brave new world, but rather to a third breathtaking possibility: the end of the dispersion of the Jewish nation and its final return to the Land of Israel – in other words, Zionism.

The first harbingers of the Return were Jews from Eastern Europe who arrived in Palestine not to pray and study, or to die and for ever sleep in its sacred soil, but to work the long-deprived land and revitalize it. In 1870, an agricultural school was established near Jaffa; a few years later, a village optimistically called Petach Tikvah ('Gateway of Hope'), was founded, on several hundred malarial acres of the coastal plain, by a handful of eager young Romanian Jews who were, in no way at all, equipped to cope with farming in general, with the Palestinian climate in particular, with the country's Arab inhabitants, or with its corrupt Turkish officials. 'Gateway of Hope' was, therefore, not a success. But the gallantry of its founders, and their burning desire to reclaim and redeem the Land, fired the imagination of Baron Edmond de Rothschild in Paris; he bailed Petach Tikvah out, set it on its feet, sent experts to direct it and kept it going. Petach Tikvah was soon joined by a cluster of other similar Jewish settlements — all of which bravely faced the same realities, invested the same determination, owed their existence to the Baron's paternalism (and the shrewdness of his overseers), and all of which carried, like banners, the same kind of ringing names: Rishon Le'zion — 'The First in Zion', Nes Ziona — 'Zion's Standard', Yesud ha-Ma'alah — 'Start of the Ascent'. Most importantly, all were, in fact, outposts of the Return, manned by men and women who came to be known as members of the First Aliyah, this being the Hebrew word for ascending, or going-up to Zion (a synonym for Jerusalem), and thus the contemporary Hebrew word for a wave of immigration.

The Second Aliyah, which settled in the Land between 1904 and 1914, was something else. Acknowledging the heroic role, as bridgeheads, of the first colonies, the young people of the Second Aliyah (which eventually brought some 50,000 European Jews to Palestine) carried with them — as befitting rebels against discrimination and exploitation — a radical credo: self-reliance, self-defence and, wherever feasible, self-sufficiency. No more planter societies subsidized by someone else's coffers; no more hired Arab labour; no more mercenary watchmen. Whatever had to be done in the homeland, they would do themselves. Among their innovations were unique lifestyles and societal patterns which became hallmarks of Zionism-in-action, one such being the kibbutz, the Hebrew word for 'group' that has acquired special meaning. Israel's more than 260 kibbutzim, comprising close to 3 per cent of today's population, are fully co-operative, economically independent and absolutely egalitarian communities; their members own no private property, receive no salaries and participate in all major decision-making and budgetary allocation. Food, housing, education, medical care, pocket money, holidays in Israel (and, when the kibbutz has had a good year, abroad) are all provided. Over the past decade, kibbutzim have turned increasingly to industry though they are still primarily agricultural.

Inevitably the present-day kibbutz is a fairly far cry, materially, even organizationally, from its precursors, established when the century was young and of which the prototype was Deganiah (the 'Cornflower') founded in 1909 on the southern shore of the Sea of Galilee. But the basic idea has not changed. Co-operation is also the outstanding feature of another form of rural group living, also pioneered by the Second Aliyah. The moshavim (of which the first was Nahalal) are villages made up of members who live with their own families in their own houses and work their own land, while sharing heavy farm equipment and collectively marketing their produce. Among the attributes which made the moshav more appealing to many of the immigrants who settled in Israel after 1948 was the fact that the individual family is usually the basic unit, often with as many as three generations on a single homestead. Some 450 moshavim (almost 4 per cent of the population) are spread out across the country.

Given Israel's history, the foundation of Hashomer can probably be regarded as the most important of the tangible Second Aliyah contributions. Forerunner of the Israel Defence Forces, Hashomer ('Watchman' in Hebrew) was born in 1907, in an ill-lit Jaffa room, when a circle of pioneers, in their high-necked Russian blouses, perched awkwardly on upturned orange crates, solemnly swore loyalty to the Jewish national cause and to each other, thereby founding a secret society to protect isolated Jewish settlements from Arab marauders. Of that distant night, one of the Watchmen, Yitzhak Ben-Zvi (who became Israel's second President), later wrote: 'We felt we were standing before Mount Sinai at the Giving of the Law ... we knew that words could not rebuild the nation, only our deeds....' The egalitarian approach, the overall informality of dress and address, the marked regard for the individual soldier that typify Israel's armed forces are rooted in the philosophy and the aspirations of the Second Aliyah, and bear the imprint of its ideology.

Yet another of the Second Aliyah's self-imposed tasks was for immigrants to abstain from the comfortable languages of their childhood and to speak only Hebrew, a consummation devoutly wished for in particular by an obsessive Lithuanian immigrant named Eliezer Ben-Yehuda. The metamorphosis of the stately tongue of the Prophets into Hebrew flexible enough to deal smoothly with rock-'n'-roll, high tech, genetic engineering, boxing, the plastic arts and space travel was, of course, not a simple matter. Ben-Yehuda meticulously compiled a dictionary which he hoped incorporated all of the words needed for contemporary living (including the word for 'dictionary') and began to speak only Hebrew himself, making his wife and children follow suit. His eldest son was, reputedly, the first child in modern times to learn Hebrew as his native tongue. In 1948, Hebrew became the official language of the State of Israel; even today it is constantly being enriched, chiefly by the Hebrew Language Academy which is charged with devising and selecting new words and, more often, with adapting old ones for current usage.

*   *   *

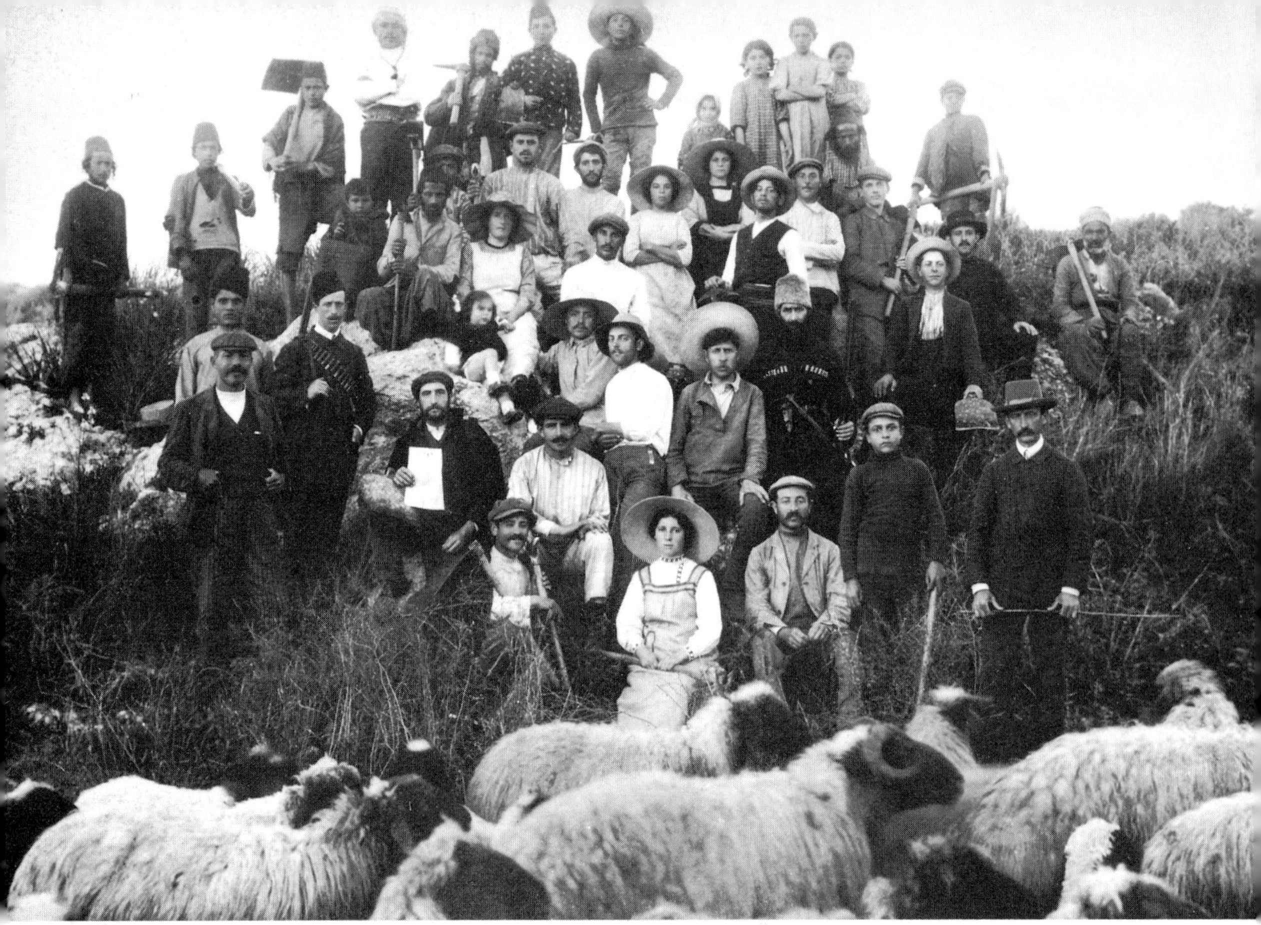

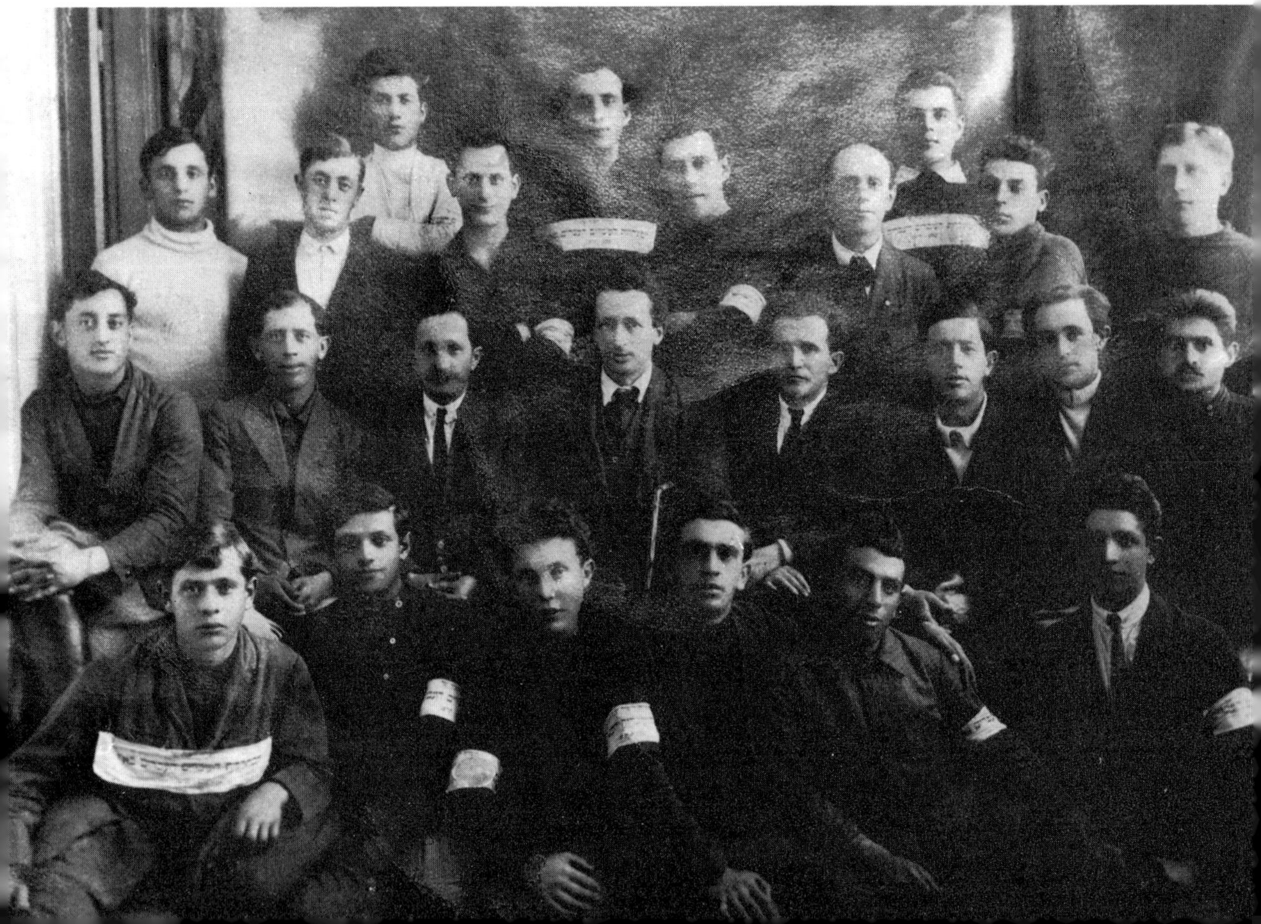

13 Opposite top: A group of early Zionist pioneers, their families and livestock, somewhere in the Land in the opening years of the twentieth century.

14 Opposite below: Yitzhak Ben-Zvi, David Ben-Gurion and Joseph Sprinzak in 1923, at the 2nd Congress of the Histadrut, the Jewish Federation of Labour established to 'care for the social, economic, cultural and trade union interests of the workers'.

15 Right: Eliezer Ben-Yehuda, 1910. In 1881 he wrote: 'Hebrew did not die of exhaustion; it died with the nation. When the nation revives, it will live again.'

16 The original 1906 building in Jerusalem of the Bezalel Academy of Arts and Design, named for the builder of the Ark of the Covenant (*Exodus* 36:2).

Although the first pioneers left Eastern Europe for Palestine in 1881 and 1882, in the West little was known about them. There the surge of interest in the Return was both epitomized, and triggered, by a handsome, elegant journalist slated to become a legend in his own short lifetime. Dr Theodor Herzl, born in Budapest in 1860, a product of the Austro-Hungarian Empire, a lawyer by training, a columnist and dramatist of some panache who was very much a man of the world, had been sent to Paris as correspondent for a prominent Viennese newspaper. Life in the City of Light was glittering, easy and interesting; it was not until the Dreyfus Affair of 1894 that Herzl awoke to the full implications of being a Jew. Alfred Dreyfus, a Jewish captain serving with the French General Staff, had been falsely accused of spying for Germany, publicly disgraced and sentenced to exile on France's terrible Devil's Island. Herzl, who witnessed the trial and heard the French mob scream 'Death to the Jews' in a country in which Jews had already been free for 100 years, was horrified – and alarmed. If this could happen in Paris, it could happen anywhere! The time had come, he declared, for the Jews to settle, a nation among nations, in a state of their own.

He expanded this idea in *The Jewish State*, a small book he published in 1896 (which not many people read), presenting his plan in minute detail including the kind of flag the new state should have, the languages to be spoken and the wages to be paid to the manual workers who would be among the first to arrive. He wrote:

We must not visualize the exodus of the Jews as a sudden one. It will be gradual, proceeding over decades ... labour will create trade, trade will create markets and markets will attract new settlers ... every man will go ... at his own expense and his own risk ... the very creation of the Jewish state would be beneficial to the neighbouring lands....

Initially, Herzl was not sure exactly where his Jewish state should be located; later, he became convinced that only the Land could answer the deepest Jewish needs, evoking a mass response to his call. On the whole, however, European Jewry thought his plan extreme, not to say lunatic, and the response was slow to come. Frantically seeking support for his ingenious proposal that the Jews help ease the by-now dire financial situation of the Ottoman Empire in return for a charter for Jewish settlement in Palestine, Herzl encountered rejection after rejection. Finally, he summoned representatives of the Jewish people to attend a national assembly which would

17 Theodor Herzl. In 1898 the settlers were in the doldrums, their struggle for existence draining, but Herzl's inspiring presence in the Land gave them new hope.

make it possible to bring into being the state he seemed unable to create alone.

On 29 August 1897, in the old Municipal Casino of Basle, Switzerland, Herzl presided over the First Zionist Congress. He had personally arranged the proceedings, carefully chosen the venue, asked the 200 Zionists who attended to wear full evening dress (which most did), and approved the opening benediction. In this address, he said: 'Zionism is the return to Judaism even before the return to the Jewish Land.' And, after the Congress, he wrote in his diary: 'In Basle I founded the Jewish state. If I said this today in public, I would be met with derision. In five years perhaps, but in any case in fifty, everybody will understand it.' At the Congress, he established the World Zionist Organization and was elected its President. In 1899, he founded an economic instrument, a national bank, for developing his non-existent state – the Jewish Colonial Trust, eventually to become Israel's powerful Bank Leumi. Nothing deflected Herzl from his desperate attempt to get the Charter, to raise the funds he thought essential and to see his glorious dream come true.

By 1901, little had happened: he toured the Land and met the Kaiser there; he was received in Constantinople by the Sultan and in Russia by the Tsar's Minister of the Interior; and he was given an audience by the King of Italy and the Pope. But no one was willing to help, and when he appeared in 1903 at the Sixth Zionist Congress with the alternative suggestion (British at source) that the Jewish state be located in East Africa, the overwhelming majority of the Zionists also turned him down. Africa would not do, though for the exhausted Herzl's sake a delegation was picked to go and take a look. Heart disease, overwork, stress and wrenching disappointment, however, took their toll of him; in the summer of 1904, Herzl died. He asked to be buried in Vienna until such time as the Jewish people would transfer his remains to the Land. In 1949, he was reinterred on Mount Herzl in Jerusalem. The words 'If you will it, it is no fairy tale,' served as the epigraph of Herzl's futuristic Zionist novel, *Old-New Land*; they have lost none of their relevance in the Jewish state which he foresaw – and fathered.

By 1914, the days of the Turks in Palestine were numbered; having entered World War I on Germany's side, having never been well-disposed towards the Jews and now actively suspicious of them, the Turks launched on a rampage calculated to rid the Ottoman Empire of this potentially 'unreliable' element. Expelling the entire population of Tel Aviv (the all-Jewish town founded in 1910 on the sand dunes outside Jaffa), deporting such future Israeli leaders as David Ben-Gurion and Ben-Zvi, the Turks hunted down, imprisoned, flogged and, when possible, hanged whatever members of Hashomer fell into their hands. Diminished, weakened and preyed upon, Jewish farms began to fail; typhoid raced through the settlements and starvation threatened the roughly 50,000 Jews left in the Land. But despite the Turkish terror, pro-Allied sentiment found its outlets: in the northern settlement of Zichron Ya'akov, an underground cell calling itself Nili (acronym of the Hebrew words for 'The Eternal One of Israel Does Not Lie') secretly collected information for the British under the leadership of Aaron Aaronsohn, a noted botanist who ran a minuscule research station on the coast. In time, the Turks discovered Nili, arrested Aaron's sister Sarah and tortured her until, rather than break, she shot herself. Sarah Aaronsohn's suicide spelled the end of Nili – regarding which the Yishuv ('The Community' as the Jews of Palestine called themselves prior to statehood) had anyhow been sharply divided; many believed that, if further enraged, the Turks might be driven to damaging the frail Zionist enterprise irreparably and that all possible provocation should be avoided. There was, however, complete agreement on, and total commitment to, the Allied cause, a consensus which resulted by 1917 (among other things) in Jewish units fighting as Jews for a Jewish homeland – for the first time in millennia.

The Jewish Legion, consisting of three battalions (one made up entirely of Jews from Palestine), operated within the British army under its own, and British, colours. Its first unit – formed in Egypt, in the crowded British barracks in which over 1,000 refugees from the Yishuv were allowed to shelter – was the jointly conceived idea of two remarkable Russian Jews, dissimilar in almost everything except the boldness of their imaginations, their iron wills and their unqualified certainty that if the Jews wanted to reclaim Palestine as their national home, then, as in the past, they would have to fight for it and, more than that, be known to have done so. Joseph Trumpeldor was a good-looking, professional soldier who had lost an arm in the 1904 Russo-Japanese war; one of the few Jewish officers to serve with the Tsar's forces, he had even been decorated for distinguished service and valour. He was an ardent Zionist and a Socialist. Vladimir Jabotinsky was an equally fervent Zionist, a journalist, brilliant orator, poet and writer.

Both were to enter Israeli history. Trumpeldor died leading the defence, in 1921, of Tel Hai, a northern settlement overrun by Arabs; Jabotinsky

18 Members of the Jewish Legion in Palestine.

19 Joseph Trumpeldor, Yishuv hero and commander of the Zion Mule Corps.

20 Opposite: In December 1917, Field-Marshal Viscount Allenby of Megiddo, as he became, then commander of the British Army in Palestine, humbly entered Jerusalem on foot.

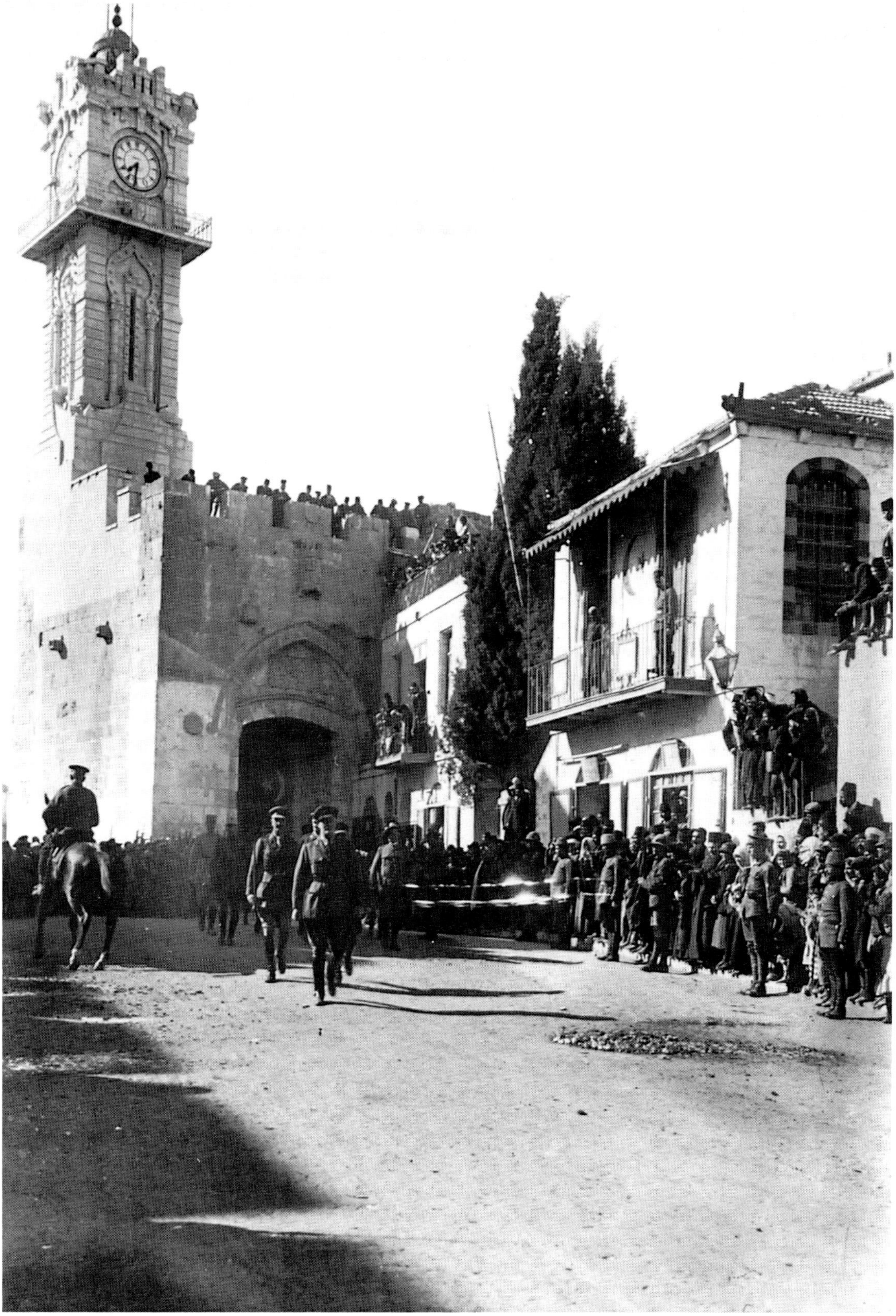

founded the militant Zionist Revisionist Movement, which became the New Zionist Organization and thus inspired the pre-state paramilitary Irgun Zvai Leumi (IZL) and Israel's right-wing Herut Party. They decided to approach the British authorities in Cairo at once with a plan for Jewish military participation in the inevitable fighting for Palestine. The British listened, agreed in principle, and suggested a mule transport unit to operate somewhere on the Turkish front. The delegation from the barracks was somewhat taken aback, but decided to seize the day and agreed. Its unglamorous name notwithstanding, the Zion Mule Corps, relentlessly drilled by Trumpeldor, flying the blue-and-white Zionist flag, duly took part in the bloody *débâcle* of the Gallipoli campaign and, in 1916, was disbanded. But Trumpeldor and Jabotinsky were not to be fobbed off with what Jabotinsky labelled 'a donkey battalion'; they renewed efforts to get British consent to something larger and more suitable. No one was interested, except a small group of influential British Jews and Dr Chaim Weizmann, who was already a Zionist leader of standing, about to play a crucial role in ensuing developments. At last, the British consented and the Jewish Legion was formed; some of its men were Mule Corps veterans, but most were Russian-Jewish immigrants to Great Britain who, as aliens, were exempt from British conscription. Recruiting went on also in the United States and Canada, and finally accounted for a total of 5,000 men under arms.

In February 1918, Jabotinsky himself one of their officers, the Legionnaires marched through London's East End, home for so many of them, heads high, bayonets fixed, on their way to the front to fight in Palestine against the Turks. By the time the British had acquiesced to the merciless demands of the Yishuv that it too be permitted to join in the triumphant advance World War I was almost over. Just before hostilities ended, a battalion of Palestinian Jews was at last formed and, in a modest ceremony held outside a Tel Aviv synagogue, the flagbearers of the 40th Royal Fusiliers proudly accepted the scarlet banner of Hashomer, upon which was written the words: 'In blood and fire, Judea shall arise.'

The Turkish collapse was complete. In October 1918, the Ottoman Empire admitted defeat, thus inaugurating a relationship between the Yishuv and various governments of Great Britain which was to endure for three decades – from the Balfour Declaration of 1917, in which Britain pledged support of 'a Jewish National Home in Palestine', up to 14 May 1948, when the British mandate over the Land terminated.

CHAPTER 3

From Balfour to Ben-Gurion

On 2 November 1917, a letter was delivered in London to Lord Rothschild, who had submitted the official request for it. Signed by British Foreign Secretary Arthur James Balfour, it read in part:

I have much pleasure in conveying to you, on behalf of His Majesty's Government, the following declaration of sympathy with Jewish Zionist aspirations.... His Majesty's Government view with favour the establishment in Palestine of a national home for the Jewish people and will use their best endeavours to facilitate the achievement of this object....

Considering its importance, the letter was singularly devoid both of style and specificity and, what's more, in the spirit of the times, constituted a promise concerning territory that was not yet Britain's to apportion. But those few dry, vague sentences – known since as the Balfour Declaration – opened the way to the Jewish state which would be voted into being just three decades later.

Among the dramatis personae connected with the issuance of the Declaration, two must be singled out: Lord Balfour and Chaim Weizmann, men who could hardly have been more dissimilar but who shared an understanding of the imperative nature of the Zionist cause. Lord Balfour died in 1930 and never saw, or even knew about, the State of Israel; Chaim Weizmann was the State's first President. For a moment in time, however, they shared the stage of history.

The Declaration, the first British undertaking of responsibility towards the Zionist movement, carried the signature, and the blessing, of a highly educated, deeply intelligent British aristocrat, born in Scotland in 1848, steeped from early childhood in the Old Testament and, consequently, possessed of a profound interest in the Jews, in the Return and eventually in

Foreign Office,
November 2nd, 1917

Dear Lord Rothschild,

I have much pleasure in conveying to you, on behalf of His Majesty's Government, the following declaration of sympathy with Jewish Zionist aspirations which has been submitted to, and approved by, the Cabinet.

"His Majesty's Government view with favour the establishment in Palestine of a national home for the Jewish people, and will use their best endeavours to facilitate the achievement of this object, it being clearly understood that nothing shall be done which may prejudice the civil and religious rights of existing non-Jewish communities in Palestine, or the rights and political status enjoyed by Jews in any other country"

I should be grateful if you would bring this declaration to the knowledge of the Zionist Federation.

Yours,

Arthur James Balfour

21 The Balfour Declaration.

Dr Weizmann. Balfour once said:

> The ideal that most moves me is that Christendom ... is not unmindful of the service which the Jews have rendered and that we desire ... to give them the opportunity of developing in peace and quietness ... those great gifts they have been compelled to bring to fruition ... in countries which know not their language and belong not to their race.

He valued, he added, this involvement above all others in a fifty-year career which included service as Prime Minister.

Chaim Weizmann, born in 1874, in a townlet in the Pale of Settlement, studied chemistry in the Russian city of Pinsk and went on to train in eastern Prussia, Berlin and Switzerland. For much of his life, he managed to combine science and statesmanship, valuable and profitable industrial discovery with fervent and effective Zionism. Offered a good laboratory in England, he settled there, gradually coming to admire profoundly British democracy, liberalism and moderation, attributes which came to characterize his political career, gaining for him the long-time leadership of the World Zionist Movement and earning him the distrust of its more militant elements. In 1918, he headed the Zionist Commission sent to Palestine by the British Government to advise on settlement, to assess the lay of the Land in general and, sadly, to learn that, 'The Balfour Declaration, which made such a stir in the outside world, had never reached many of [General] Allenby's officers, even those of high rank. They knew nothing about it.' Not disheartened (he remained convinced of British good faith for many testing years), Weizmann felt that it was essential to seek immediate rapport with the Arabs.

That same year, in a desert encampment in Transjordan (then still part of Palestine), Weizmann met with Emir Feisal, son of the Sharif of Mecca whom the British had promised to make king of the Arab countries freed from Turkish rule. A photograph of the two stately, robed, look-alike figures catches the chemistry between them. Weizmann asked for the Emir's support, elaborating on the ways in which the Return would inevitably improve the Arab lot – something that Feisal at once accepted. A year later, the Emir went further; backed by his omnipresent adviser, T. E. Lawrence (otherwise known as Lawrence of Arabia), Feisal signed an agreement with Weizmann which called 'for all necessary measures ... to encourage and stimulate the immigration of Jews to Palestine'. Its Preamble emphasized that both parties were aware of 'the racial kinship of the Arab and Jewish peoples' and that both realized the need for 'the closest possible collaboration'.

* * *

22 The 1918 Zionist Commission: in addition to Dr Chaim Weizmann (standing, second from right), Aaron Aaronsohn (bareheaded, on the steps); next to Weizmann, Major W. Ormsby-Gore, later to become British Colonial Secretary.

23 Chaim Weizmann (left) with Emir Feisal, 1918, at the latter's desert headquarters.

At the Paris Peace Conference of 1919, it was decided that Palestine should become a mandated territory, to be administered by a trustee or mandatory government; in the following year, Britain was chosen for this role. Confirmed by the League of Nations in 1922, formally declared in effect in 1923, the mandate was far more clearly worded than the Balfour Declaration to which it referred: the mandatory power was 'made responsible for placing the country under such political, administrative and economic conditions as will secure the establishment of the Jewish National Home ...' and was required to 'encourage', not merely permit, the settlement of Jews in the Land; to 'facilitate Jewish immigration'; and to recognize 'an appropriate Jewish agency' to help the Palestine administration with matters concerning the National Home and the interests of the Jewish population. Other clauses safeguarded the civil and religious rights of non-Jews; made English, Hebrew and Arabic official languages; and provided for enactment of a nationality law which would make it easy for Jews, immigrating to the Land, to acquire Palestinian citizenship. Neither the letter nor the spirit of the mandate could be misunderstood; though if needed, international sanctioning of the Balfour Declaration was further strengthened, in 1922, by the Joint Congressional Resolution on the Jewish National Home which represented the US Government's enthusiastic endorsement: '... the Jewish people are to be enabled to recreate a national home in the land of their fathers ..., which will give to the House of Israel its long-denied opportunity to re-establish a fruitful life and culture in the ancient Jewish land....' It was signed by President Harding.

Once agreed upon, the job ahead began to look formidable; it was one thing to lay down policy, another to implement it. Almost from the first day, the Palestine administration made clear to the Jews – and therefore also to the Arabs – that it was out-of-sympathy with, not to say irritated by, the complicated and bewildering mission entrusted to it. The Zionists, too, found themselves facing daunting obstacles and disappointments: the land was barren, stripped of forests and top soil, some of the more fertile regions already lopped-off and closed to Jewish immigration and settlement; Transjordan, the major part of Palestine, had been presented by the British, in 1921, to Feisal's brother Emir Abdullah (Feisal himself receiving what is today Iraq) as consolation for having been chased out of Arabia by Ibn Saud; and another sizable stretch of land, this time in the north, was ceded to the French, who held the mandate for Syria. But neither Turkish mismanagement of the Land nor lost territory were anywhere near as serious as the virtually instantaneous whittling-down of the mandate.

In 1920, a number of events took place which together – and separately – symbolized the intricacy of the Palestine puzzle. A distinguished British Jew, Sir Herbert Samuel, and one of the godparents of the Balfour Declaration and a leading member of the Liberal Party, was appointed British High Commissioner to Palestine. For the first time in 1,850 years, a Jew would rule over the Land of Israel; the Yishuv was beside itself with pride, with joy and with gratitude to the mandatory power. Sir Herbert's initial official visit, when he arrived in Jerusalem, was to the main synagogue in the Jewish Quarter. It was a Saturday; to avoid offending the observant, he went on foot, slowly, through the dim twisting alleys of the Old City to take part in a Sabbath service that included the opening lines of a chapter from Isaiah: 'Comfort ye, comfort ye, my people, saith your God. Speak ye comfortably to Jerusalem and cry unto her that her warfare is accomplished, her iniquity pardoned.' Many years, and recriminations later, the High Commissioner was to write of that morning: 'People wept. One could almost hear the sigh of generations.'

But Jerusalem's warfare was far from accomplished. For the new post-war breed of Arab nationalists, who had come into being throughout the Middle East and who were almost as anti-British and anti-French as anti-Zionist, the idea and budding facts of the Jewish National Home were anathema and, more than that, served as themes of a unifying and reverberating war-cry. The first major outbreak of anti-Jewish violence came even before Sir Herbert took office, even before the mandate itself was ratified. In 1920, the Arabs began a series of attacks on the little Jewish settlements in northern Galilee, in one of which Trumpeldor was mortally wounded. The looting and bloodshed quickly spread to the Old City of Jerusalem, where an Arab crowd, worked up by Arab nationalists, went berserk, burning Jewish homes and shops, killing and raping Jews. The British Military Governor sealed the Old City – and the fate of Jews in it – and ordered the arrest of the Legionnaires (Jabotinsky among them) and Hashomer members organized in a self-defence corps, frantically trying to rescue the trapped victims.

The pogrom lasted three days. In 1921, rioting broke out again, in bloodier form, in Jaffa; again in 1922, and in 1929 133 Jews – men, women and children – were mutilated and killed, chiefly in Hebron, Safed and Motza. The British eventually restored peace, but clearly were not about to defend the Jews forcefully enough or punish the Arabs with real severity. One result of the deteriorating situation was the Yishuv's decision to disband Hashomer

24 Vladimir Jabotinsky, out of the Legion and jailed for having complained directly to Allenby about British bias, arriving in London in 1920.

and create in its place a self-defence organization which would be broadly based, able to function in many directions and depend not so much on individual valour as on the backing and involvement of the entire population. Thus was born the Haganah (Hebrew for self-defence), which accompanied, and helped ensure, the growth of the Yishuv until it, in turn, was disbanded upon the formation of the Israel Defence Forces (IDF) in 1948. It was still not in a position, however, to ward off the worst of the Arab riots, which began in 1936, lasted for three years, took the lives of 2,287 Arabs, 520 Jews and 140 Britons, and forced a final assessment by all concerned of their respective stands.

But broken promises, dashed hopes, even the successive British measures taken to curb the momentum of Zionist development, did not halt its progress. Slowed down, wearied, alarmed by continuing Arab hostility – which included the destruction of crops and thousands of newly planted trees – the Yishuv ploughed ahead and developed its agriculture, specializing in citriculture and mixed farming; built roads, drained swamps and turned Tel Aviv into a bustling fair-sized town; and launched industrial projects including exploitation of the chemical resources of the Dead Sea. It also invested time, money and energy into its intellectual future. In 1925, Lord Balfour came to attend the opening ceremony of the Hebrew University in Jerusalem; the student body was small (today it numbers over 16,000), but Chaim Weizmann, also a major architect of Jewish higher education in Palestine, was eloquent in his explanation of the rightful place of a university in the National Home. Within a few years, a scientific research institute, later to bear his name, was founded by Weizmann amidst the orange groves of the coastal plain; and in Haifa, a much-praised technological institute had been turning out students since 1924. Other fields also flowered: in 1936, the Symphony Orchestra's gala opening concert was held in Tel Aviv under the baton of no less than Arturo Toscanini; the Hebrew theatre was active and Hebrew literature doing nicely.

Paradise regained? Hardly. If the British White Papers, negative statements and braking actions ignored the true possibilities of Palestine, the mandatory power, and its representatives in the Land, were even blinder to the suddenly heightened, urgent Jewish needs of the 1930s. All innocence lost, we now know the fearful, implausible sequence of subsequent events, but, in 1934, the shadow of Nazism that slanted across Germany was threat enough for German Jews, who were given to understand that they did not, after all, belong there; that they had no inherent rights or privileges; that they could

25 Lord Balfour at the moving and ceremonial foundation-laying of the Hebrew University on Mount Scopus, Jerusalem 1925.

be tormented, expelled from school, have their property stolen and their dignity trampled underfoot, because they were members of an inferior and evil race, regardless of the fact that they had been wholly integrated into German society for so long.

The children came to the Land first (largely through the good offices of two middle-aged ladies, Recha Freier, a German Jewess, and Henrietta Szold of Baltimore), sent by reluctant, fearful parents; then whole families left for Palestine. Nearly 70,000 German Jews arrived in 1935 alone, part of what is known in Israel as the Fifth Aliyah which brought nearly 165,000 Jews to the country between 1933 and 1936, increasing the Jewish population to some 400,000, or about 30 per cent of the total.

The 'Yekkes', as the German Jews were nicknamed (for the leather jackets they wore with their well-pressed shorts and sun helmets), changed the face of the Yishuv; not as intoxicated by the romance of Zionism as the Russian and Polish pioneers had been, far more sophisticated and worldly, they improved and Westernized whatever endeavour they entered, and in their own stolid way, they were just as adventurous. Some joined kibbutzim; others, having to set aside careers as writers, lawyers, engineers or scientists, took to agriculture and animal husbandry, establishing model farms and poultry coops; still others, preserving the manners and meticulousness of earlier existences, became skilful plumbers, polite waiters, even energetic and efficient bricklayers. The Yishuv, in general, welcomed and appreciated them, laughing at the trouble the Yekkes had in learning Hebrew, at their heavy Teutonic accents, at their incomprehensible jokes and their abiding formality. In the meantime, the Jewish presence in the Land acquired a new look, tidier, more middle class; Beethoven and Mozart flowed from Tel Aviv balconies; in cafés, beer vied with glasses of tea; German magazines, *lieder* and movies bespoke a nostalgia unfamiliar to former *shtetl*-dwellers.

The Arab riots intensified, preying not only on Jews but also, and later mostly, on the Arab *fellahin* or peasants, forced at gunpoint to join the gangs that roamed the Land at the command of an Arab Higher Committee, headed by the unsavoury Grand Mufti of Jerusalem, Haj Amin el-Husseini. The Mufti's influence in Palestine was considerable and regrettable; tutored and aided by the Nazis, he warned shrilly that the Arabs would be displaced by the onslaught of Europeans, never mentioning the astronomic prices being paid for the purchase of Arab land. When these warnings were not enough, he called for a general strike: no Arab in Palestine would go to work until all Jewish immigration stopped and the transfer of land ended. He also

26 Henrietta Szold, founding President of Hadassah (the Women's Zionist Organization of America), also headed Youth Aliyah which, from 1933 on, resettled and rehabilitated thousands of underprivileged or endangered youngsters, such as those shown with her here.

27 The notorious Mufti of Jerusalem (far left), after testifying before the Palestine Royal Commission of 1936.

demanded a government with a parliament which would be elected by 'the people'. In short, annul the Balfour Declaration; cancel the mandate!

The British, not averse to solving the Palestine problem by indirection, were not prepared for downright repudiation; although boldness was not a feature of British policy-making in the 1930s, the Palestine administration refused to give way to the threats. It responded with 30,000 troops, martial law and emergency regulations, all of which temporarily cooled Arab fervour while the Jews proceeded to fill the vacuum left by the strike. Jaffa port stopped functioning, so Tel Aviv acquired a jetty, obviously an embryonic harbour; Arab bus drivers quit their vehicles, so Jewish drivers took over, plying the ambushed, sniper-ridden roads and becoming national heroes; Arab produce went unharvested and unmarketed, so Jewish farmers worked longer hours meeting the challenge. But the three years of the riots were hard to take: the casualties, the cortèges regularly winding their way through the streets, the continuing wanton sabotage, the charred trees.

Of course, there were also the silver linings: neighbourly relations, never entirely interrupted by the riots, always resumed upon restoration of what, in the Middle East, passed for normality. Jewish and Arab orange growers got together to open foreign markets, whenever possible; a number of Arab trade unions came into being with the help of the Histadrut, the General Federation of Labour; Arab working conditions were, and remained, better than in the Arab states; and in the mixed towns such as Haifa, Arab and Jewish municipal councillors managed to work together. The closest co-operation, however, was always rural and, though the political crises remained untouched by this, it was important that, even in the worst of times, attacks on Jewish settlements were usually carried out by armed bands assembled and dispatched for the special purpose, rather than by local villagers.

The Zionist leadership, unhappily weighing alternatives, ordered the Haganah to limit itself strictly to self-defence. A cardinal consideration was not to give the British any excuse for curtailing Jewish immigration, nor any easy opportunity for revoking the Haganah's semi-legal status. Some groups within that organization refused to accept the shackles, seceded and went their own militant way. Eventually the Haganah, still adhering to national discipline, acquired a permanently mobilized force, empowered to act throughout the country. The credit for the important transformation belongs to a couple of colourful, unconventional and courageous men.

Yitzhak Sadeh, creator and first commander of the Haganah's Palmach (from 'Plugot mahatz' or 'striking companies'), and, even before that, one of

28 Yitzhak Sadeh, creator and first commander of the Palmach.

29 Orde Wingate: 'I have seen the young Jews in the kibbutzim. They will provide a soldiery better than ours. We have only to train it.'

the Yishuv's most imaginative, experienced and innovatory soldiers, might (like Trumpeldor who so greatly influenced him) have stepped from the pages of an adventure story. Decorated for bravery in the Russian army in World War I, he served with the Red Army, studied philosophy and philology at a Crimean university, distinguished himself as a weightlifter and wrestler and, in 1920, learning of Trumpeldor's death, left for Palestine, where he helped to found a labour battalion that he named for Trumpeldor. When the riots broke out in 1936, he proposed to the Haganah that static defence be abandoned, that the Jews assert themselves militarily, and that defence in depth replace amateurish plans for each and every settlement. Eventually, as the situation worsened, the recommended field companies were formed and placed under Sadeh's command as, later, was the active, flexible, multi-purpose Palmach he envisioned. Outspoken, intuitive, articulate (as became a one-time playwright and poet), he taught the arts of warfare and command to young disciples destined, within only a few years, to lead the army of Israel – and who owed to Sadeh much of what they knew.

Captain Charles Orde Wingate, 'The Friend' as he was known in the Haganah, was altogether different. Born in India, related to Lawrence of Arabia, a professional Arabist who had served in the Sudan, he was consumed by twin passions: military science and the Bible. Like Lawrence, slight, intense, eccentric, idolized by those who fought under him, Wingate was posted to Palestine in 1936 and developed a lifelong and requited love for Zionism. About his first encounters with the Yishuv, he wrote: 'I felt I belonged to such a people'; and to the British, he recommended the formation of part-Jewish, part-British, Special Night Squads to operate against Arab terrorists, using secrecy, surprise, mobile ambushes and hand-to-hand fighting, and always taking the initiative. His unorthodox approach (known today as guerrilla warfare), his unabashed comradeship, his openly voiced high hopes for the future of the National Home, hugely appealed to Sadeh; together they rapidly made the Night Squads operational and successful. Wingate's reward from his disapproving superiors was transfer from the Land, his passport stamped 'Not Allowed To Enter Palestine'. He went on to train and lead troops operating behind enemy lines in Burma and died there in a 1944 aircrash. No one present at the opening of a Jewish Sergeants' Course, held in a kibbutz in 1938, ever forgot hearing Wingate say, sternly, 'Remember, we are here to found a Jewish army!'

Its faith in the efficacy of White Papers and Commissions being strong, in

1936 the British Government sent to Palestine a Royal Commission headed by Lord Peel in the hope that these six gentlemen would come up with a solution to the Palestine problem. Although the Arabs refused to appear before it, in 1937 the Commission issued a 400-page report reiterating the 'primary purpose of the mandate' as being promotion of the establishment of the Jewish National Home and stating that the Land's much-debated absorptive capacity ('No room to swing a cat' was the way one Colonial Secretary put it) could only be increased by further immigration and the influx of capital. However, the report went on to advocate that, since Arab opposition rendered present arrangements unworkable, Palestine be partitioned into two states, one Jewish, one Arab, with a permanent British mandate over certain areas. After much heart-searching, the Zionist movement gave qualified support to the basic design, though many Zionists utterly rejected the idea of a state which, instead of the original 45,000 or 50,000 square miles, would be reduced to a mere 2,000 square miles – or, to one-fifth of the country west of the Jordan, i.e. one-twentieth of the territory covered by the Balfour Declaration. The Arabs, still incited by the Axis, would have nothing to do with the whole thing. The mandatory government announced its acceptance of the report but, in trying to work out the details, yet another Commission reduced the whole thing to absurdity and the Government withdrew its endorsement of partition.

Note should be taken of the period: Neville Chamberlain was the British Prime Minister, 'Peace in Our Time' the password; Czechoslovakia was out of the way, so why not get the Palestine people together and clear that problem up too? In February 1939, the British convoked a Round Table Conference in London inviting representatives of the Jews, of the Arabs and, which was a bit odd, of the neighbouring Arab states. The Arabs refused to meet the Jews; the British talks with both parties did not amount to anything, or so it appeared by the time everyone got ready to go home. But before the Conference broke up, the British unveiled a new policy, made official in the White Paper of May 1939. This White Paper, which made clear that the Arab Higher Committee had indeed won the political struggle over Palestine, limited Jewish immigration to a total of 75,000, even from Nazi Germany, after which immigration was to be subject to Arab approval; it empowered the High Commissioner to prohibit the transfer of land in specific and extensive areas; it provided for establishment within ten years of a Palestine government, based on the actual population of the country in which the Jews

The Peel Commission Partition Plan, July 1937

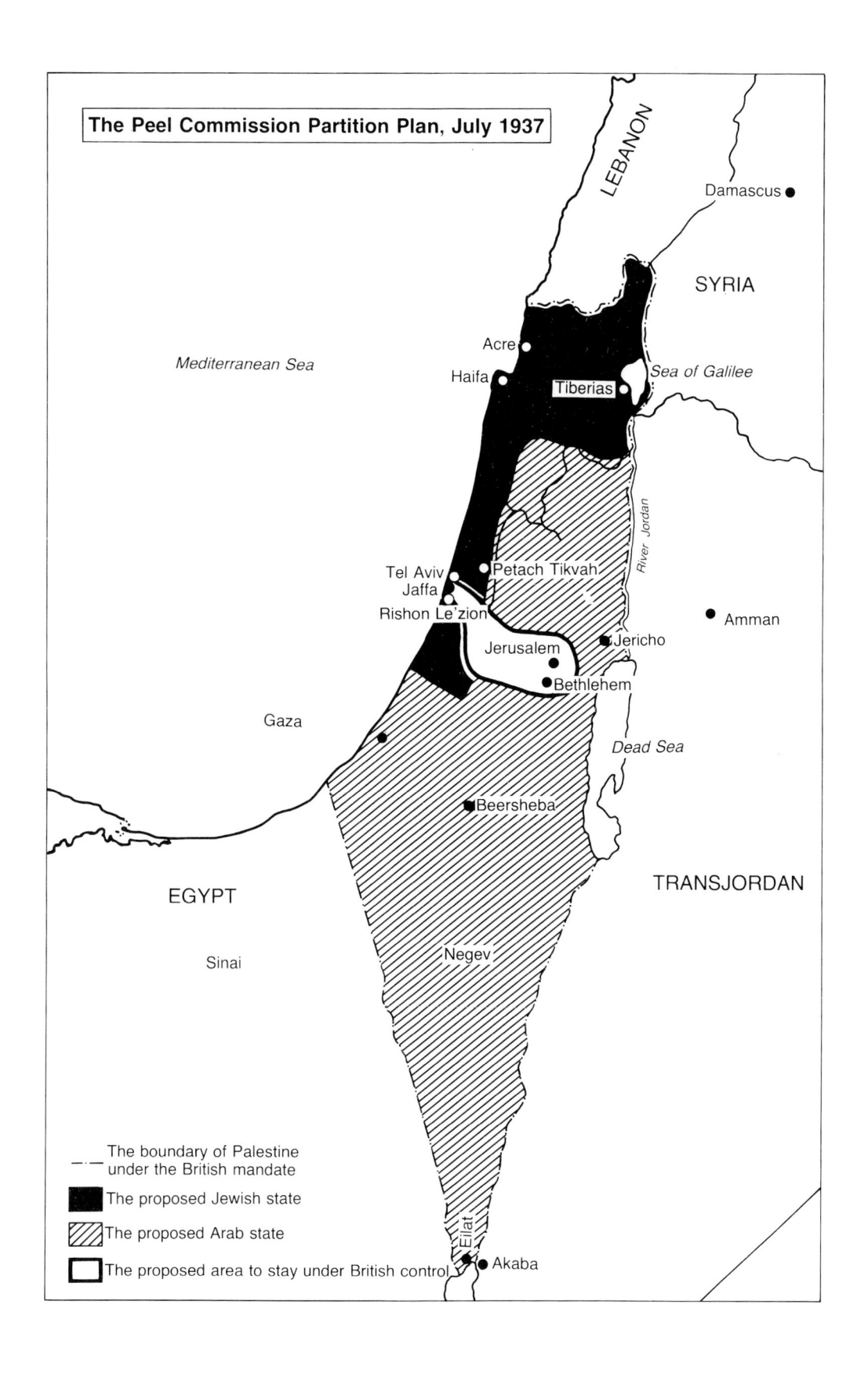

- — · — The boundary of Palestine under the British mandate
- ■ The proposed Jewish state
- ▨ The proposed Arab state
- ☐ The proposed area to stay under British control

were not to exceed one-third of the whole; and it ordered disbandment of the Haganah.

In brief, the 1939 White Paper, albeit politely and again without explicitly revoking the Balfour Declaration and the mandate, denied the rights of the Jews as such to Palestine, relegating those Jews already there to permanent minority status in a territorial ghetto. No Zionist leader, not even one as moderate as Chaim Weizmann, could possibly accept these terms, but nor did the Arabs and nor did the Permanent Mandates Commission which unanimously held that the White Paper was 'not in accordance' with the construction put on the mandate by the mandatory power and the League Council. The League of Nations, however, was not in good shape itself; the outbreak of World War II resulted in suspension of its activities and, though the League never gave legal sanction to the White Paper policy, the British could, and did, press on with its implementation.

The Yishuv was aghast, infuriated, but mostly desperate. Nazi seizure of western Poland had sent millions of Jews searching for escape, shelter, maybe even lasting haven somewhere. For the Jews of Palestine, these fugitives were not distant objects of pity; they were parents, brothers, sisters, friends, people wanted nowhere else whom they yearned to take in. A hopeless tug-of-war began: the Jewish Agency trying to rescue as many Jews as fast as possible; the Palestine administration doling out the precious certificates in accordance with its new quota. The saga is well known; a reminder or two should suffice: the cockleshells, unseaworthy and crowded, illegally bore their cargoes of men, women and children to the shores of Palestine only to be deported to Mauritius in the Indian Ocean, or imprisoned elsewhere. Possibly the most indelible story of the early attempts to deliver European Jews from the Nazi dragnets is that of the tiny SS *Struma*, whose 764 exhausted passengers waited for nearly two months in the port of Istanbul in the winter of 1941 hoping to get Palestine visas. In the end, only the children were allowed to proceed, but even that decision came too late; the Turkish authorities had already turned the *Struma* back into the Black Sea where she sank, taking to their death all but one of the refugees.

Nineteen forty-one was also the year of German victories, including those in the Middle East. The Mufti of Jerusalem was ensconced in Berlin, waiting to join the Nazis when they rolled into Palestine; in Iraq, there was a pro-Nazi revolt; and throughout the Arab states, in mosques and coffee shops, there was cheerful talk of how it would be when Hitler and Mussolini finally arrived. The Yishuv, unalterably committed to the fight against Nazism,

30 Jewish Legion veterans join a protest march against the British White Paper, Jerusalem 1939.

31 In October 1939 forty-three Haganah members were imprisoned for illegal arms possession. They included Moshe Dayan (extreme right), who in 1941 lost an eye while on a secret British commando mission.

unalterably committed to save Jewish lives, searched for a formula which would reconcile the profound collective need to co-operate with the British against the Germans and, at the same time, continue, undiminished, the battle against the White Paper. That formula was found by the Chairman of the Jewish Agency, David Ben-Gurion: 'We shall fight the war as if there were no White Paper,' he said, 'and we shall fight the White Paper as if there were no war.'

CHAPTER 4

The Jewish State

The Yishuv's participation in the war effort took many forms, all requiring enormous, and maddening, persistence. British opposition to the active, visible presence of Palestinian Jews in the armed forces was based mainly on the justified assumption that, if they were permitted to fight under their own colours and contribute collectively to Nazi defeat, the Zionists would almost certainly demand changes in the White Paper once the war ended. The Yishuv's intense desire to fight the Nazis directly was therefore not only discouraged but, even if only partially yielded to, always likely to be rendered ineffectual. When the Jewish Agency rushed to organize mass registration of volunteers for war service, and close to 90,000 men and 50,000 women put down their names, the British made a condition: volunteering had to be on a parity basis – one Jew, one Arab. The Arabs were not exactly waiting on line to serve, so the Yishuv kept up the pressure. Finally, the British agreed, but for a long time denied Palestinian Jews the privilege of front-line fighting; and when the formation of all-Jewish units was eventually allowed, they were not formally known as such. It was only in 1944, due largely to the personal interest of Winston Churchill, that a Jewish Brigade Group was created which fought in Italy under the blue-and-white Zionist flag and served in Europe within the framework of the British Army of Occupation.

Ultimately, however, the fortunes of war overrode British rigidity. In the Western Desert, Empire troops were pushed back by Rommel's army; it looked as though Egypt, and then Palestine, might fall to the Germans. Urgent needs had to be met: food, drugs and essential equipment for thousands of Allied soldiers throughout the Middle East. For the first time, the skills, capabilities and allegiances of the Yishuv became assets for the mandatory power; the Jewish civilian population of the Land went on wartime footing: scientists, meteorologists and surgeons provided expert services;

technicians repaired cannons, ships and bridges, built roads, runways and radio installations in Iraq, Bahrein and Cyprus.

Throughout its own war to fight the war, the Yishuv was no less profoundly preoccupied by an anguished search for ways and means of rescuing Jews from the vast, virtually impregnable fortress that was now Europe. One suggestion after another, each more daring than the last, was put forward by the Jewish Agency, each in turn rejected by the British. In 1942, the Jewish Agency proposed the dispatch, behind the lines in Nazi-held territory, of hundreds of parachutists charged with setting up rescue operations, rallying the starving dehumanized Jews with the sight and sound of caring messengers from the Land, encouraging sabotage and revolt and, in this way, perhaps even helping to overthrow the Germans. Moreover, because many Palestinian Jews came from the Balkans and could mingle, intimately and safely, with the Balkan people – and since anti-Nazi underground organizations already existed in all Balkan countries – emissaries like these could also take and bring priceless information and rescue fallen Allied pilots. The British again said 'No'.

But in 1943, even fear of Jewish post-war claims could no longer obscure the merit of the Jewish Agency's scheme; the military situation in the Balkans was approaching disaster, and pro-Allied saboteurs and reliable liaison with Balkan partisans were of the utmost importance. British Intelligence was persuaded that the Agency's offer must now be accepted. However, not hundreds, not even scores of air-borne operatives were used; just thirty-two Palestinian Jews – two of them women – at long last were dropped into Europe, into Romania, Hungary, Italy, Slovakia, Austria and Yugoslavia. Seven, among them the two women, did not return; one, Hannah Szenes, a dark-eyed girl, originally from Hungary, who wrote poetry ('Blessed be the match that is consumed in kindling flame'), was caught in Hungary, imprisoned, tortured and – as her mother waited nearby to see her – shot. She became a national heroine in the Land, symbol of the Yishuv's response to what was happening in Europe, her name adorning one of the leaky, rusty boats of the succouring fleet with which, from the summer of 1945 to the end of 1947, some 70,000 immigrants would be brought from Europe into Palestine – in defiance of the law, in dead secret, under frightful conditions and the constant hostile surveillance of British agents.

Gradually, though not yet fully, the truth regarding the fate of European Jews began to seep out. A disbelieving world was forced to realize that

32 Moshe Sharett, Director of the Jewish Agency Political Department, later Israel's Foreign Minister and briefly Prime Minister, proudly presenting a flag to the Jewish Brigade on the Italian front, March 1945.

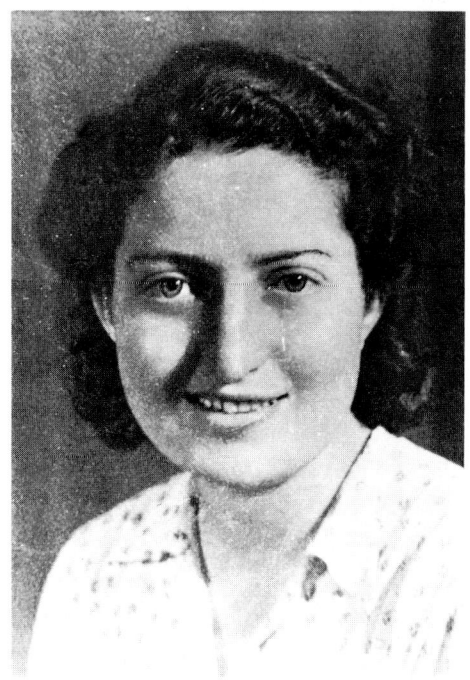

33 Hannah Szenes, the Jewish Agency operative dropped into the Balkans who did not return.

34 Pain and fear etched on their faces, illegal immigrants of the 1940s were prepared to confront further danger, deprivation and indignity in order to make their way to the Land.

Hitler's monstrous design had almost been completed, that six million Jews had been murdered by unspeakable means and that a remnant remained, leftovers of a catastrophe of such dimensions that, half a century later, survivors of the death camps, old men and women, would still be testifying – in courts, through books, on film – that, yes, however dreadful, it had all really taken place. In the summer of 1945, when horrified and sickened Allied troops liberated the camps, food, clothing and medicine were rushed from all over the civilized world to the dazed and disabled men and women who had experienced what no group of people had ever experienced before – and lived. Everything possible was done for them – with one exception: no government said it wanted them, would cherish them, would take all and any who wished to become its citizens.

In the summer of 1945, the battle lines were drawn, the struggle (*ma'avak* in Hebrew) between the mandatory power and the Jews of the Land, focusing on immigration, reached a stage of irreversibility; uneven sides faced each other stonily across an abyss. If confusion ever existed about the issues involved, it was now dispelled; everything was clear to everyone. As early as 1942, in an emergency conference held in New York, Weizmann, Ben-Gurion and other Zionist leaders called for an opening of the gates of Palestine, with the Jewish Agency being given control of immigration and 'the necessary authority for upbuilding the country ...', and urged '... that Palestine be established as a Jewish Commonwealth integrated in the structure of the new democratic world'. The Arabs took longer with their statement of intent; in 1945, Egypt, Saudi Arabia, Syria and Lebanon finally declared war against the Nazis and, with British aid, formed the Arab League, which at once declared Palestine to be an Arab state as promised by the White Paper of 1939. The third party to the conflict also left its position in no doubt: the British Labour Party, which came into power after the war, had long been considered, and described itself, as pro-Zionist. But the Yishuv's refusal to abandon insistence on bringing Jews to Palestine, the accompanying increasing tensions and violence, the assassination (in 1944) by two Palestinian Jews of Lord Moyne, the Resident British Minister to Cairo, and the bitter personal antagonism of the British Foreign Secretary, Ernest Bevin, rendered this description archaic. When, in a letter to British Prime Minister Clement Attlee, US President Harry Truman appealed for admission to Palestine of an additional 100,000 'displaced persons' (DPs) from the camps, the British refused to consider his request, suggesting instead that, since the Americans were so concerned with the plight of the Jews, an Anglo-American

Committee of Inquiry study the problem.

In retrospect, it is possible that had Attlee agreed to Truman's proposal, the current Middle Eastern situation would have been very different. But he did not, and an Anglo-American Committee was duly established, the eighteenth fact-finding body to deal with Palestine. Diligently it went the European rounds, interviewed DP's, spoke to representatives of the British and US Armies of Occupation, to leaders of British and US Jewry, and in February 1946 arrived in the Land where it heard more testimony, not least the Jewish Agency report encapsulating Jewish history from the destruction of the Second Temple. While the Committee deliberated, the situation in Palestine worsened: the certificates permitted by the White Paper were used up and all official immigration stopped. The British announced a new policy: 1,500 certificates a month, if the Arabs agreed. When the Arabs said 'No', the British gave the Agency the certificates anyhow, but the ludicrous allocation solved little. Jewish resistance stiffened; the British, unable – despite a blockade and use of destroyers, aircraft and tanks – to break the will of the Yishuv, began to view the Jews *en masse* as political offenders, which helped explain the virtually unlimited powers handed to British soldiers, detectives and constables.

The Anglo-American Committee of Inquiry Report, published in May 1946, accepted neither the idea of immediate independence nor that of partition. 'Jew shall not dominate Arab and Arab shall not dominate Jew,' it proclaimed, and reminded everyone that the Christian churches too had a right in the country, thus sounding a new, if not particularly welcome, note. Its practical proposal was a trusteeship under the newly constituted United Nations. It further recommended admitting the 100,000 refugees and removing restrictions on land sales to Jews. The British government, faced by standard Arab threats, announced that it would only consider admitting the 100,000 when both sides disarmed. Nobody around was anxious to become a trustee or understood what this meant; the DPs still languished in their enclosures; the Yishuv exploded. The matter of self-restraint was no longer academic; splitting off from the Haganah, with which it had been briefly united, the right-wing Irgun Zvai Leumi (its mentor the long-exiled Vladimir Jabotinsky, its commander Menachem Begin), and the much smaller, more extreme Stern Gang, openly revolted against the British, while official Jewish leadership expressing itself through the Haganah permitted the use of force in the cause of immigration, but prohibited the singling-out of British personnel.

When news came of the British rejection of the Anglo-American Committee's recommendations for the 100,000 certificates, the Haganah wrecked bridges and railways throughout the Land. The British then rounded up and jailed most of the Yishuv leadership, raiding and ransacking settlements in their frantic search for hidden arms. The extremist groups followed with flamboyant and deadly action, blowing up government offices in Jerusalem's King David Hotel, killing nearly 100 Britons, Jews and Arabs. The British decreed curfews for days on end, ordered detentions, passed death sentences and started shipping to Cyprus the illegal immigrants on whose pitiable behalf all this was happening.

By 1947, the British position was untenable; bullets and bayonets used against Palestinian Jews and DPs were not going to solve anything nor be tolerated much longer, either in Britain or by world opinion. In Palestine, British troops were now ghetto people: forbidden to associate with Jews, and terrified of the retaliation meted out for every action against the Yishuv by one of the three underground organizations; the Palestine administration was locked up in heavily guarded compounds; and habeas corpus was a thing of the past. Martial law was no fun for the ruled, but it made life impossible for the rulers. Nor was illegal immigration the sole area of Jewish defiance; the creation of Jewish settlements in prohibited areas also carried the message of the Yishuv's denial of the White Paper. In short, 'untenable' was an economical way of saying that, for the British, remaining in Palestine was exceedingly unpleasant, inordinately expensive and not worth the trouble. Let the United Nations see what it can do, said Mr Bevin in the House of Commons in February 1947.

So UNSCOP (the United Nations Special Committee on Palestine) entered the post-World War II lexicon. The Committee, like its immediate predecessor, came to Palestine, talked to everyone – except the Arabs who refused to acknowledge it – met with leaders of the Arab states, journeyed to Germany and Austria, after having been treated, unfathomably, by the British to a display of the harrowing consequences of the Government's decision to force the return to Germany (using combat troops) of the over 4,500 illegal immigrants (they included 2,000 children) who arrived in Palestine in July 1947 aboard an old American ship renamed the SS *Exodus*. On 31 August, from the former Palace of the League of Nations, UNSCOP issued its report recommending, as the Peel Commission had done, the termination of the mandate, the partition of Palestine into an Arab state and a Jewish state, a special arrangement for Jerusalem, and economic union for

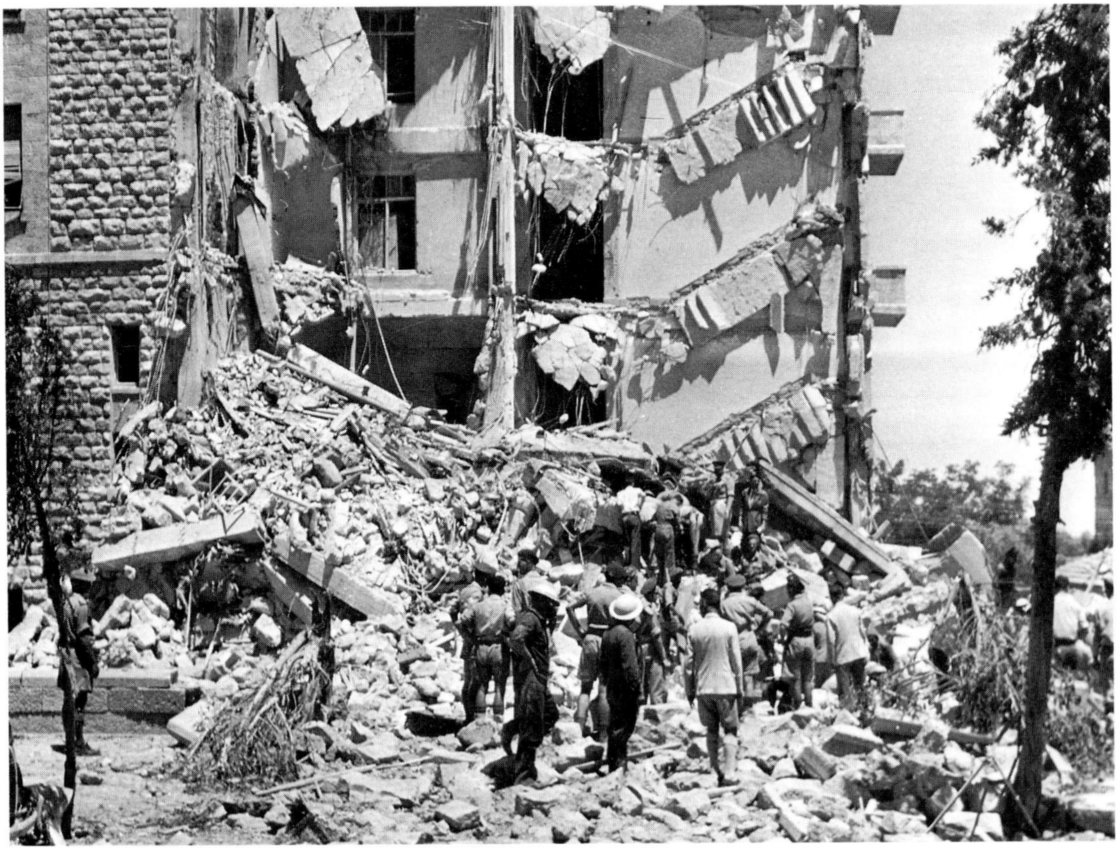

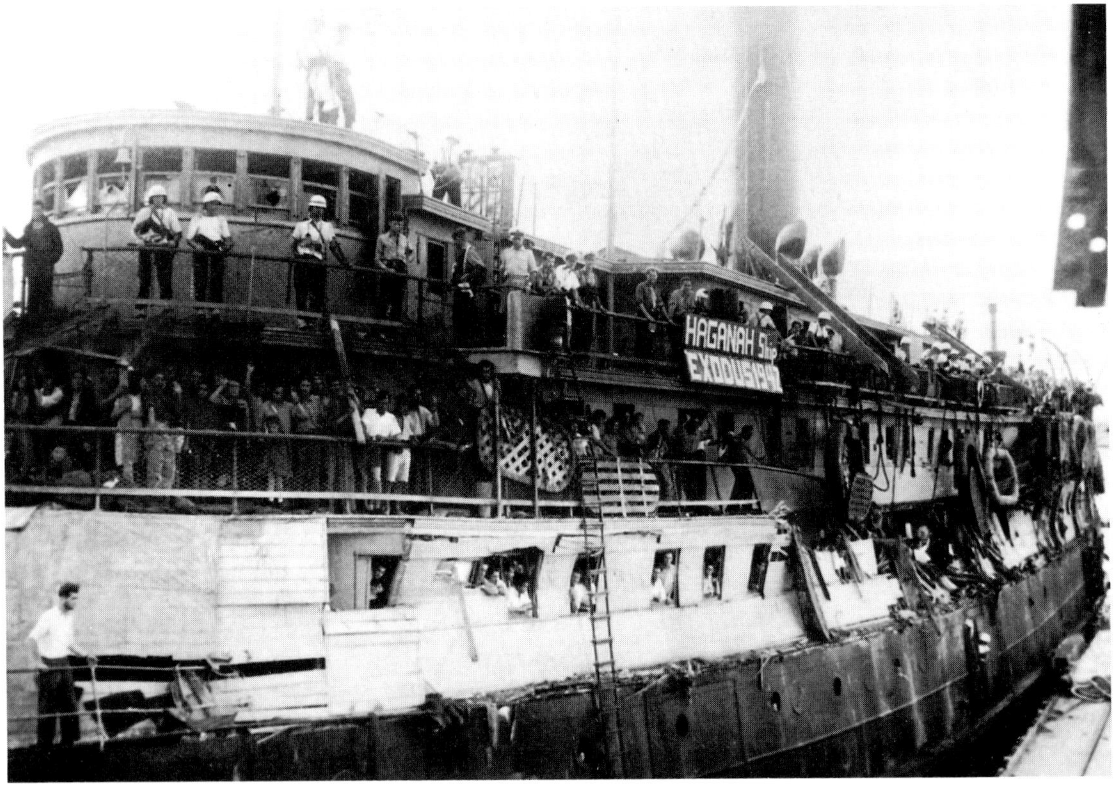
HAGANAH
EXODUS

35 Opposite top: The debris left behind by the Irgun Zvai Leumi explosion of a wing of Jerusalem's King David Hotel, which housed the British Military HQ, July 1946.

36 Opposite below: The best-known of the immigrant ships to reach the land, *Exodus 1947*, whose passengers – penned in wire cages – were sent back to Hamburg, Germany.

37 Above: Part of the British police poster describing Stern Gang and Irgun Zvai Leumi members who escaped from Acre fortress in 1947. Menachem Begin, later Israeli Premier, is bottom row, fourth from left.

the whole country. By 29 November, the UNSCOP Majority Report (a minority report upheld by India, Yugoslavia and Iran suggested a federal Arab-Jewish state), slightly amended, was accepted by the UN General Assembly in New York. Thirty-three countries voted 'Yes'; thirteen voted 'No'; ten, including Great Britain abstained. The United Nations had created its first ward; speaking through it, most of the world had authorized the realization of the dream of Jewish independence, liberty and refuge.

As for implementation of UN Resolution 181 (11), familiar stances were again adopted: the Arab states announced that they would oppose partition by force; the Jews, with mixed feelings, accepted it; the British, upon whose co-operation its success depended, said that, since both sides had not agreed to the UN Resolution, the British Government would have no part of the proceedings, would not let UN representatives into the country while the mandate was still operative, and fully intended to remain in exclusive control until 15 May 1948. Ernest Bevin's rancour was most apparent in the British refusal to abide by the Resolution's requirement that the mandatory power evacuate a port (and surrounding area) for the reception of immigrants.

The news of the passing of the Resolution reached Palestine at 1 a.m. on the night between the 29th and the 30th of November. In the compound of the Jewish Agency building in Jerusalem, hundreds of people, British soldiers among them, joyously held hands, embraced each other, sang and danced. Golda Meir, a ranking member of the Jewish Agency Executive, recalled the scene:

... from the balcony of my office I spoke for a few minutes ... not really to the mass of people below me ... it was ... to the Arabs. 'You have fought your battle against us in the UN,' I said, 'the UN ... have had their say. The partition plan is a compromise; not what you wanted, not what we wanted.... Let us now live in friendship and peace.'

That day, an Arab ambush killed seven Jews; next day, the Arabs of Palestine declared a three-day strike. The celebration only lasted a few hours and not everyone in the Yishuv danced or sang. No one knew then that the war which had already broken out would last nearly sixteen months, consist of close to forty military operations, and involve mobilization of what amounted to the entire Jewish population of the Land (in May 1948, about 650,000 people) – of whom a staggering 1 per cent were to be killed – to meet the assault of five regular Arab enemies plus a million Arabs of Palestine. No one knew this, but then no one knew whether the state would ever come

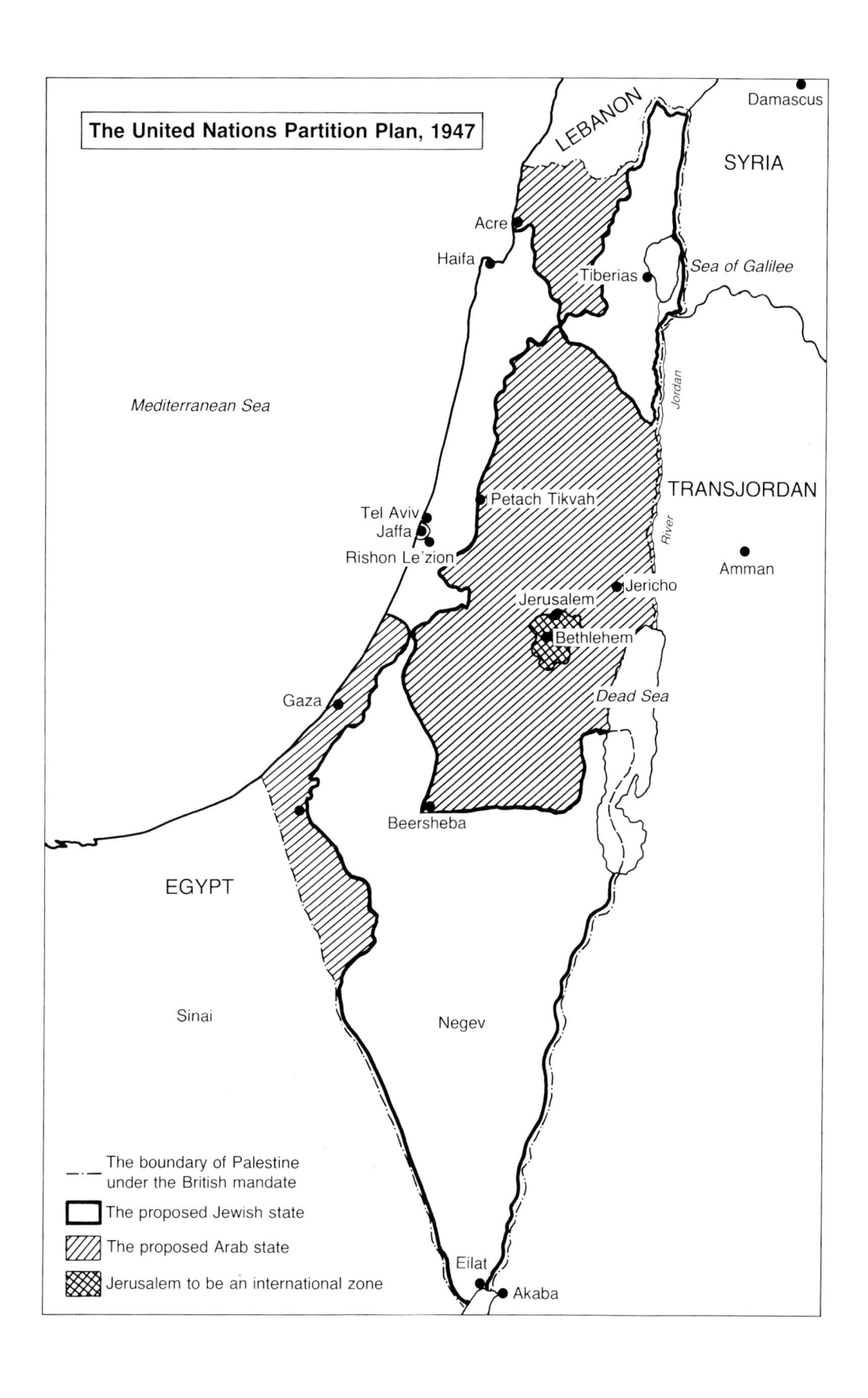

The United Nations Partition Plan, 1947

--- The boundary of Palestine under the British mandate
☐ The proposed Jewish state
▨ The proposed Arab state
▩ Jerusalem to be an international zone

into being, or, having been born, would survive its birth.

The British and the Arabs were as good as their word. Until May 1948, the British, seemingly bent on the creation of chaos, engaged in highly selective attention and inattention. Insofar as immigration was concerned, the administration adhered strictly to White Paper legalities, as though nothing had changed; DPs without certificates, bound for the land, were hunted, seized and deported to camps in Cyprus. However, when it came to government stores, installations and essential records such as land registry deeds (Ben-Gurion went in vain to the High Commissioner to ask for these), it turned out that whatever was not handed to the Arabs or destroyed was simply 'lost'. The Arabs, for their part, switched from random raids and killings to increasingly focused attacks on Jewish settlements and vital roads, concentrating their efforts on isolating Jerusalem. Bolstered by British indifference to the weekly quota of murder and destruction (and even greater indifference to the vulnerability of the Jewish population), seduced by lurid descriptions of the joys awaiting them in conquered Tel Aviv, bands of Palestinian Arabs and irregulars from across the borders were on the offensive throughout the Land. As for the Haganah, driven further underground with each passing month, aware that full-scale warfare would break out as soon as the British departed Palestine's inhospitable shores, knowing precisely what hung in the balance and how meagre its military supplies — a few thousand rifles, a few hundred machine-guns, a mixed bag of other weapons, nine small planes — stepped up its arms procurement, mainly in Czechoslovakia, and hurriedly trained new immigrants with wooden rifles and dummy bullets. It vowed to hold on to all Jewish settlements, regardless of their size or the ferocity of the attack mounted against them — which was almost, though not quite, accomplished. Above all, the road from the coastal plain to Jerusalem had to be kept open or Jerusalem, the core of the Land, and its 100,000 Jews already under siege, might be cut off and captured, the only access to the rest of the country being a winding forty-mile mountain road, dominated by the Arabs who controlled most of the hilly regions of Palestine. The noose had to be loosened, and soon.

A UN Implementation Committee came, looked around and returned to New York to wonder aloud whether the Jewish state had any chance of making it; were there no alternatives, considering the turmoil and toll? In April 1948, Ben-Gurion sent a convoy into battle for Jerusalem's life. On the first vehicle were scribbled the words: 'If I forget thee, O Jerusalem, let my

38 One of the longest of the precious convoys that reached beleagured Jerusalem during the weeks preceding the establishment of the state.

right hand lose its cunning.' That convoy got through but was the last for a long time, the longest time, in fact, that Jerusalem had been besieged since the Crusades. There was no food, petrol or electricity, and one bucket of water per family; when the British finally left, there was also a shortage of news, perhaps, under the circumstances, the greatest deprivation.

On 14 May, General Sir Alan Cunningham, last British High Commissioner to Palestine, left Jerusalem's Government House in full dress uniform, flew to Haifa, took a salute from a company of the Palestine Police, shook hands with Haifa's Jewish mayor and Arab deputy mayor, boarded a waiting British cruiser and, from its deck, watched the Union Jack lowered. The evening before, he had broadcast a farewell message: 'It would be easy ... to say sometimes "here we did right", and no doubt at other times, "there we did wrong" ... the way ahead has not always been clear ... in this respect we are more than content to accept the judgment of history.' And he prayed that peace might come to Palestine, even at that late hour.

The British withdrawal left the Land devoid of air or sea mail, tax collection, car registration, functioning health controls, even much local currency. The thirty years of the mandate came to an end, abruptly, humiliatingly and arbitrarily, doing little justice to the high hopes that had accompanied the beginning of the great venture, or to the many men of distinction and ability associated with it. The long-term legacy of some of the best of British tradition would, in the future, be incorporated into that of the State of Israel, but on the day of Sir Alan's embarkation, this could not be taken for granted. In fact, the breach was to heal with unforeseeable rapidity; although Great Britain abstained from voting, in 1949, for Israel's admission to the UN, early that year Ernest Bevin announced *de facto* recognition and, shortly afterwards, the appointment of Britain's first diplomatic representative to the Jewish state.

At exactly 4 p.m. that Friday afternoon, in Tel Aviv's small art museum on the boulevard named for Baron Rothschild, against a background of flags and a picture of Theodor Herzl, in the presence of some 200 deeply moved people who rose to their feet, in a short ceremony (the time and place of which had been kept secret till then), David Ben-Gurion read out Israel's Proclamation of Independence. The 979 Hebrew words, which took about twenty minutes to read, stressed the unbroken link between the Land and the Jewish people; referred to Herzl and the Balfour Declaration; declared that the state would be called Israel; that it would be 'open to Jewish

39 Friday, 14 May 1948: General Sir Alan Cunningham sails from the Land, closing the thirty-year drama of the British mandate.

40 Friday, 14 May 1948: David Ben-Gurion proclaims Israel an independent state. Its first ordinance: 'All laws enacted under the Palestine White Paper, 1939 ... are hereby declared null and void.'

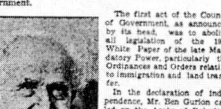

41 A newspaper headline announcing the birth of the new state.

immigration and the ingathering of exiles'; that it would 'promote the development of the country for the benefit of all its inhabitants' and be based on liberty, justice and peace 'as envisaged by the Prophets of Israel'; and that it would loyally uphold the principles of the UN Charter. It called upon the United Nations to assist the Jewish people in the building of its state and appealed 'in the very midst of the onslaught launched against us ... to the Arab inhabitants of the State of Israel ... to play their part in the development of the state on the basis of full and equal citizenship and due representation in all its bodies and institutions'. To the Arab states and peoples, the Proclamation offered 'peace and good neighbourliness', and promised that the State of Israel would 'make its contribution to the progress of the Middle East as a whole'.

The traditional Jewish blessing was intoned ('Blessed be Thou, Oh Lord our God, King of the Universe, who has kept us alive and made us endure and brought us to this day'). Then, the Secretary of what was now the Provisional Government called upon those members of the Provisional State Council (evolved from the Jewish autonomous agencies under the mandate) to sign the Proclamation; the Zionist anthem, the *Hatikvah* ('The Hope') was sung; just after 4.30 p.m. Ben-Gurion said: 'The State of Israel has arisen. This meeting is ended.'

The First Zionist Congress had been grander, the decor and the clothes more elegant, but both Herzl and Ben-Gurion had felt the same need to write something afterwards in their diaries. Alone for a moment, a war for survival to be fought, endured and won, Ben-Gurion quickly wrote: 'At 4 p.m. Proclamation of Independence. I am filled with foreboding.'

Outside the museum, among the notices being posted was one issued by the Haganah:

1. Shelters must be dug in all residential areas and the orders of Air Raids Precautions officers must be obeyed.
2. Mass gatherings in open areas and streets must be avoided.
3. Every assistance must be given to the commanders of the security forces in erecting barriers, fortifications, etc.
No panic. No complacency.
Be alert and disciplined.

CHAPTER 5

The Cost of Independence

On 15 May 1948, at dawn, five Arab armies invaded Israel, bent on destruction of the day-old state whose Jewish population, it had already been made clear, they intended to 'drive into the sea'. Each participating Arab country had its own additional war aim: Jordan hoped to regain all of Palestine, particularly Jerusalem; Iraq, her ruling dynasty related to Jordan's, sought an outlet to the Mediterranean, through Jordan if necessary; Syria coveted Galilee, with the Moslems in Lebanon casting longing looks especially at western Galilee; Egypt, largest and best-organized of the invaders, wanted not so much land as the kudos which would be attached to playing a major role – as the supreme Arab power – in the easy victory that lay ahead. No less confident of the quick outcome were Saudi Arabia and Yemen, both of which dispatched token representations. Judging by the relative numbers of men, *matériel* and equipment involved, Arab optimism, on the face of it, was not unreasonable. None the less, the War of Independence was neither quick nor easy, and when it was over, more than 1,000 square miles had been added to the territory originally allotted to the Jewish state.

For brevity's sake, the war can be divided into four phases: the first, beginning on 30 November 1947, ending at different times in different places in accordance with the schedule of British withdrawals (which also varied in time and place), was characterized by the Haganah's determination not to abandon even the remotest Jewish settlement, to avoid direct clashes with the administration, and to postpone large-scale offensives against the Arabs until the British left. The second phase was the confrontation between Jews and Arabs while the British were still withdrawing and before the mandate ended. During these weeks, all of upper and lower Galilee, Haifa, Safad, Tiberias, Jaffa and parts of Jerusalem were brought under Haganah control, albeit at the cost of many casualties, the ruin of precious transport and the

42 Israeli soldiers advance in hand-to-hand, house-to-house fighting in a Jerusalem suburb, May 1948.

43 Hoisting a hand-inked Israeli flag in what would become Eilat, after a dramatic race through the desert in the final phase of the War of Independence, March 1949.

much-mourned loss of some settlements around Jerusalem. The third phase was the Arab invasion. Wingate and Sadeh's lessons paid off: the Haganah, which might have crumbled under the impact of the five-pronged Arab assault, coped with it, rebuffed it and held its own. Yigal Allon, the Palmach commander, wrote: 'If the Haganah had concentrated ... on defence ... initiative would have remained with the enemy ... the Haganah adopted a combination of defensive methods and offensive action which came to be known as "active defence"....' By June, the scoreboard showed that the Arabs had lost impetus, that the Haganah needed time to prepare for new campaigns and that everyone craved breathing space. When the UN called for a month's ceasefire beginning on 11 June, it was accepted by all with relief. That truce, as it was called, lasted for twenty-eight days and changed the tide of the war.

For Israel, the most tragic loss was the Jewish Quarter of the Old City of Jerusalem. Two weeks after the Proclamation of Independence, it fell to the 20,000 armed Arabs who had waited for weeks for the British to leave so that the Quarter's 2,000 deeply religious, unworldly Jews, their lives dedicated to study and piety, could be taken captive and the Old City, a truly glittering prize, ceremoniously handed to Jordan's King Abdullah. All through the tense winter of 1947–8, the Yishuv had feared for the Old City. From a military point of view, defence of the walled-in, one-square-mile tangle of alleys and arcades, a jumble of stone houses and sites holy to three religions, described in the Book of Psalms as a town 'built all compact together', presented a mind-boggling problem. But it was unthinkable to desert David's City. Outside its ancient walls, in the three weeks that followed the British evacuation, residents of the beleaguered New City squared shoulders to take the merciless hammering of thousands of shells lobbed at them from Jordanian and Egyptian artillery, to get used to hand grenades and mortar bombs flung into houses and streets, and to adjust to incendiary bombs dropped from planes. Morale high despite the deaths, the anxiety, the thirst and the hunger, Jerusalemites held fast. But the Jewish Quarter was not able to do so; the eighty Haganah members holed up there for months – and those who had fought their way into the Old City to try to help them – were outnumbered thirty to one, no match for the Arab Legion. Fighting house-to-house, down to their last rounds of ammunition, without food or water, by 28 May the Haganah soldiers could no longer withstand the onslaught; the Old City fell, its Jewish Quarter to become debris, its synagogues razed, its homes looted.

Most of its inhabitants were permitted to pass through to the New City, some 300 were captured; it would take nineteen years, and the Six Day War, before Jews returned to the Quarter and Jerusalem was made one city again.

Among the consolidations that took place during the ceasefire was the transformation of the Haganah into the Israel Defence Forces, including the introduction of uniforms and ranks, the disbanding of the dissident underground organizations and the inclusion of their members into Israel's army. On 31 May 1948, an Order of the Day was issued, which read, in part:

On the establishment of the State of Israel, the Haganah has emerged from the underground and has become a regular army.... Without the Haganah's experience, planning, skill ... and valour, the Yishuv could not have held its ground in the dreadful trial of arms it has had to face during these six months and we would not have attained the State of Israel.

It was signed by David Ben-Gurion, Prime Minister and Minister of Defence. Even today, and to a considerable degree, the IDF retains the Haganah's imprint – in its *esprit de corps*, in its lack of extraneous spit-and-polish, and in the absence of a dividing line between military and civilian – since all Israelis, men and women alike, serve in the armed forces (men also doing reserve duty for most of their adult life).

The fourth and last stage of the war started in July 1948 with a full-fledged decisive and victorious Israeli offensive in which enemy forces were crushed, the danger to Tel Aviv eliminated, the siege of Jerusalem lifted, the Egyptians checked in the south, the Iraqis in the east and the Syrians in the north. A second ceasefire halted the offensive. It lasted till the middle of October, afforded the IDF time to regroup, rest, reinforce units, replenish stocks and set in motion a brand new unit, Nahal (acronym of the Hebrew words for 'Fighting Pioneer Youth'), designed in part to replace the Palmach, which gave youngsters combined military training and preparation for settling the land – and later served also as a model for various developing states of Asia and Africa. By the end of this ceasefire, Israeli troops had lifted the Egyptian siege of the Negev, crushing Egyptian forces and taking the entire northern Negev including Beersheba; only one Egyptian brigade remained in Israel's south until the armistice, its young intelligence officer a major named Gamal Abdel Nasser.

War's end was in sight, though peace seemed elusive; Israel's borders were not yet defined to the satisfaction of the United Nations. In May 1948, the UN had appointed a mediator, Count Folke Bernadotte, closely related to Sweden's King and President of the Swedish Red Cross, who began at once to work out a peace plan that deviated significantly and sharply from the partition plan. It suggested, among others, that Jerusalem be disarmed and demilitarized and that most of the Negev be absorbed into Jordan in exchange for an Israeli western Galilee (ignoring the fact that Israel had already acquired this area), and that the UN supervise all Israeli air and sea ports. Bernadotte's 'compromise' proposals, wrote an Israeli historian, were 'maladroit at best but widely regarded as sinister', chiefly the 'special internationalized status' which the Count recommended for Jerusalem including the New City. In September, a group of never-identified assassins struck Bernadotte down on a tranquil street in Jerusalem; with him, died one of the UN's French observers. Despite the shock and horror of the killings, Israel could accept none of the late Count's proposals. 'What we have won on the battlefield, we will not yield at the council table,' Ben-Gurion explained to the US Ambassador.

Bernadotte's successor as mediator was Dr Ralph Bunche (subsequently awarded the Nobel Peace Prize for his labours), whose boundless patience and tact guided the immensely complex series of armistice agreements which, though falling far short of peace treaties, permitted a measure of stability in the Middle East and brought about cessation of immediate hostilities. Each agreement (with Egypt in February 1949, with Lebanon in March, with Jordan in April and with Syria in July – Iraq withdrew without any formal agreement) established demarcation lines and a commission (on which both sides were represented) headed by a chairman responsible to the UN Security Council. The question of negotiating without the UN never arose since no Arab state was willing to talk 'directly' to the Israelis. Bluntly stated, the agreements had come into existence only because Israel had pushed back the invaders; beyond tacitly recognizing this fact, the terms tended to compensate the losers. Only Jordan – which kept the Old City and added some 2,200 square miles of Palestine (i.e. today's West Bank) to its kingdom – appeared at all interested in any permanent arrangement. After the armistice was signed, King Abdullah held a number of secret talks aimed at arriving at a treaty with Israel. His belief in the importance of amity between his country and the Jewish state had been demonstrated before, although just three days prior to the invasion when Golda Meir – travelling at night disguised in the robes of an Arab woman – met him in Jordan to ask him not to join in an

44 Count Folke Bernadotte arriving in New York to report to the Security Council, July 1948.

Arab attack against the Jewish state, the King turned her down. She reminded him of promises he had made in earlier, equally clandestine meetings, to which he said, 'Ah, but now I am one of five,' asked why the Jews were 'in such a hurry to proclaim their state' and conveyed the message that he, too, would indeed wage war against them. In July 1951, he was murdered by Arab nationalists on the steps of the Mosque of Omar in the Old City, a warning to those Arab leaders who might be tempted to talk of peace – though it did not deter the President of Egypt, Anwar Sadat, from being prepared to pay the same price for the same reason exactly thirty years later.

And what of the Arabs of Palestine, a country which no longer existed though there still were, and are, Palestinians? According to Israeli estimates, between 550,000 and 600,000 local Arabs fled when war became inevitable. This was for two main reasons: they were frightened of what might happen to them under Israeli rule; and, from the first months of 1948, Arab League propagandists repeatedly advocated the seeking of temporary refuge across the borders, with a subsequent return in the wake of the triumphant Arab armies. According to UN estimates, 725,000 Arabs left. What is indisputable is that 160,000 either never took flight or, having done so, came back at once. Natural increase has since brought the number of Israeli Arabs up to 660,000. The idea that the Arabs might leave the country *en masse* and of their own volition may have been quite welcome to a large segment of the Israeli population, but the leaders of the Yishuv understood all too well the distortions and damage that would certainly result from any Arab flight – and begged the Arabs not to leave.

None the less, some 30,000 Arabs left right after the November 1947 Partition Resolution; 200,000 more during that winter and the spring of 1948; and roughly another 300,000, following the establishment of the state, in departures carried out in spurts – and with mysterious efficiency. In Tiberias, for instance, in April 1948, the entire Arab population – 6,000 men, women and children – vanished across the Syrian and Jordanian borders in a single night. In Haifa, 65,000 Arabs ran away, despite appeals by the Workers' Council asking them to remain rather than unnecessarily doom themselves to 'poverty and humiliation'; in Jaffa, 50,000 Arabs followed suit. It did not help that, on 10 April, Irgun Zvai Leumi and Stern group fighters, surrounding the Arab village of Deir Yassin on the Jerusalem road, met with resistance and killed tens of Arab civilians. Deir Yassin was turned into a convenient and durable symbol of Israeli brutality, but the lemming-like flight

45 Some Arab women and children who fled in the wake of war return in December 1949 to Acre.

of the Arabs was well under way before that tragic attack, and a still unsolved problem of immense human and political significance already forming.

Everything had to be done concurrently; the apparatus of government fully activated, made adequate to the needs of a population that, literally, increased weekly; international trade, commerce, diplomatic relations established as rapidly as possible; order restored to daily life, national and personal, lest the social fabric give way to the extreme strains imposed upon it. In the eighteen months that followed the Proclamation of Independence, over 340,000 Jews entered the Land; they came from seventy-four countries, speaking as many tongues, born into all levels and kinds of culture and development, adhering to the habits of hugely dissimilar diasporas. It was, truly, in the words of the Proclamation, the In-Gathering of the Exiles. By the end of 1951, Israel had taken in, and unto itself, 764,800 immigrants, more than doubling the Yishuv and including Jews from Poland, Bulgaria, Czechoslovakia, from the DP camps of Germany and Austria, the 50,000 Jews from Yemen — crammed into converted transport planes that made up what Israelis called 'Operation Magic Carpet' but which the Yemenites believed were the wings of eagles as written in the Bible — and from Iraq almost 93 per cent of that country's Jewish population (124,000) via 'Operation Ali Baba' airlifts.

For all these thousands upon thousands, the National Home was now a tent in one of the canvas cities which sprang up all over Israel — leaky, cold, uncomfortable in winter; hot, airless, uncomfortable in the long summer — a tent which also meant neighbours from opposite ends of the earth with whom, for lack of a common language, not even complaints or recipes could be shared, and whose ways and tastes were incomprehensible, often revolting. Many immigrants were not well or competent enough to hold jobs, many had lost the desire to work. Special medical centres had to be set up to care for the aged, the disabled, the chronically ill; room had to be made in existing schools, and new schools improvised, for the host of children starting from scratch. The Government, the Jewish Agency, world Jewry (a total of $150 million was raised in 1948 by the US United Jewish Appeal alone, half going to Israel, half to aid the Jews of Europe) — and the IDF — took care of the rock-bottom needs of the returning multitudes and got everyone fed, clothed, given pots, pans and minimal furniture, inoculated and equipped with identity cards.

Soon the tents were replaced by tin shacks which provided better shelter and more privacy, but were clustered in what were doomed to become shanty

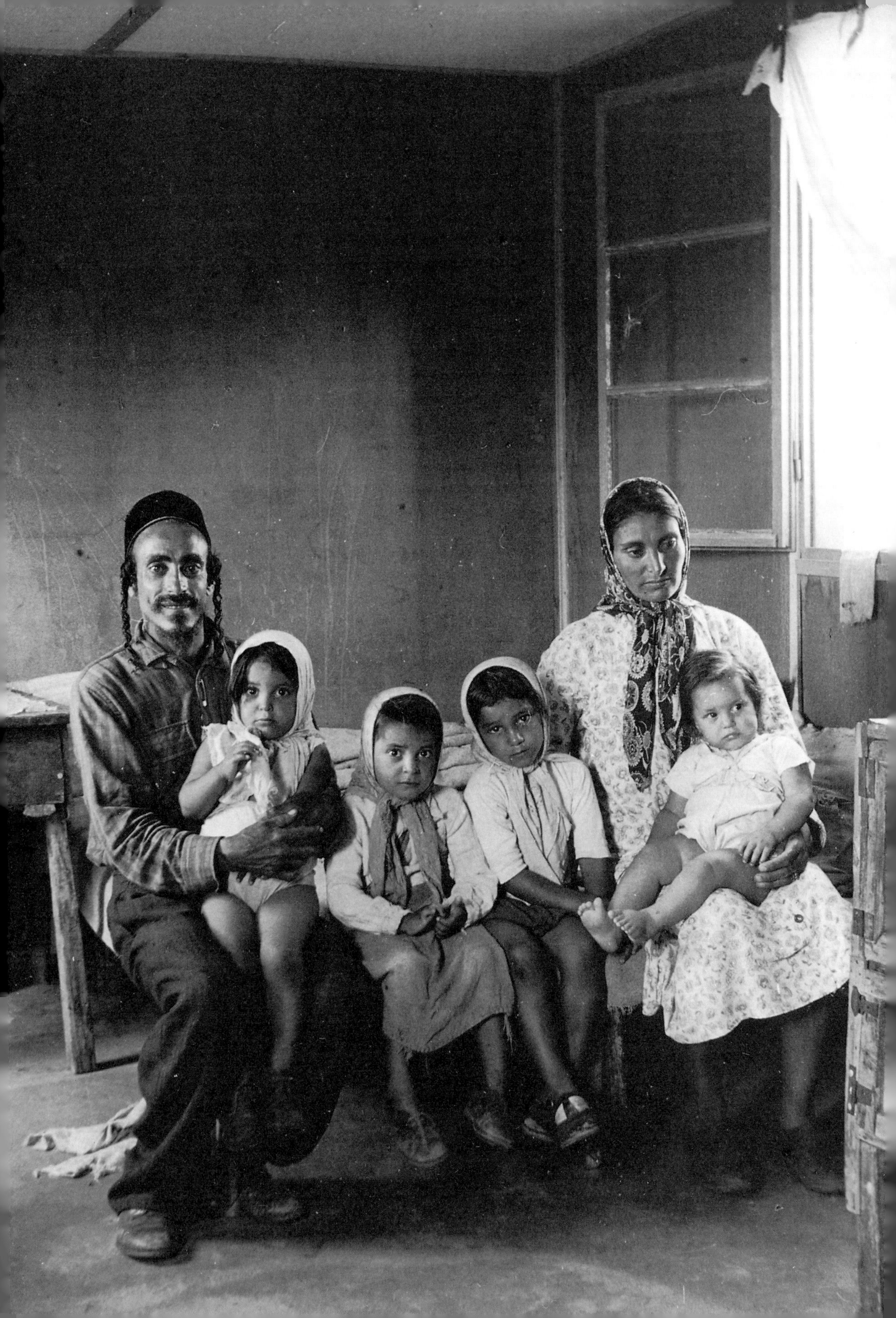

46 Opposite: A family of newcomers from Yemen: most Yemenite Jews brought to Israel via Operation Magic Carpet read and understood Hebrew and were proficient in crafts unfortunately useless in a modern economy.

47 Above: Operation Ali Baba included Jews from Kurdistan (an area divided among Turkey, Iraq and Iran), some probably descendants of Jewish exiles who settled in Assyria in biblical times.

48, 49, 50 Above and opposite: In all, 684,000 Jews entered Israel in the first three years of independence. First came the ma'abarot (transit camps) which by 1952 housed 250,000. Afterwards came development towns and new place names, among them Dimona and Yerucham in the south, Migdal Ha-emek and Kiryat Shmonah in the north.

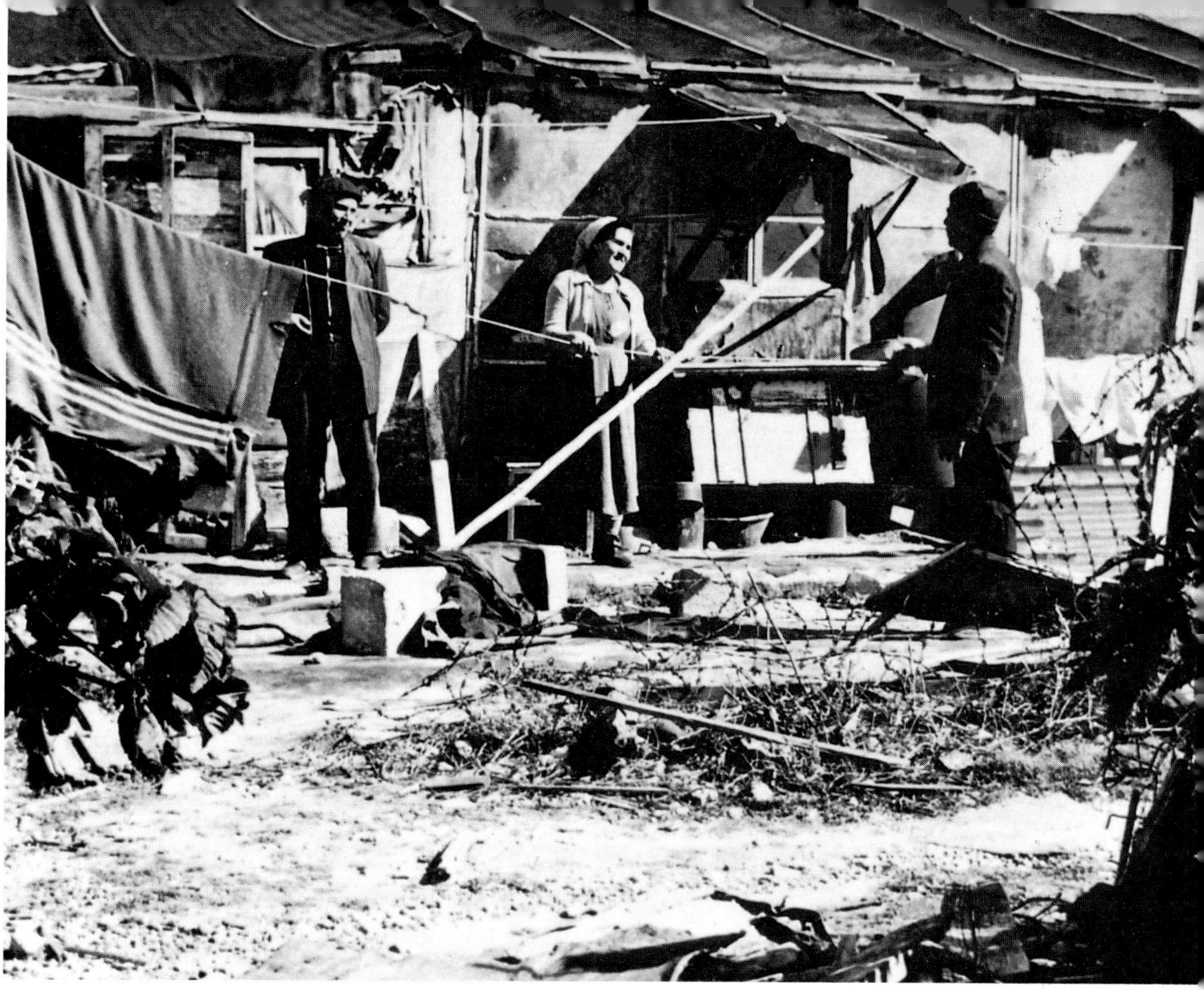

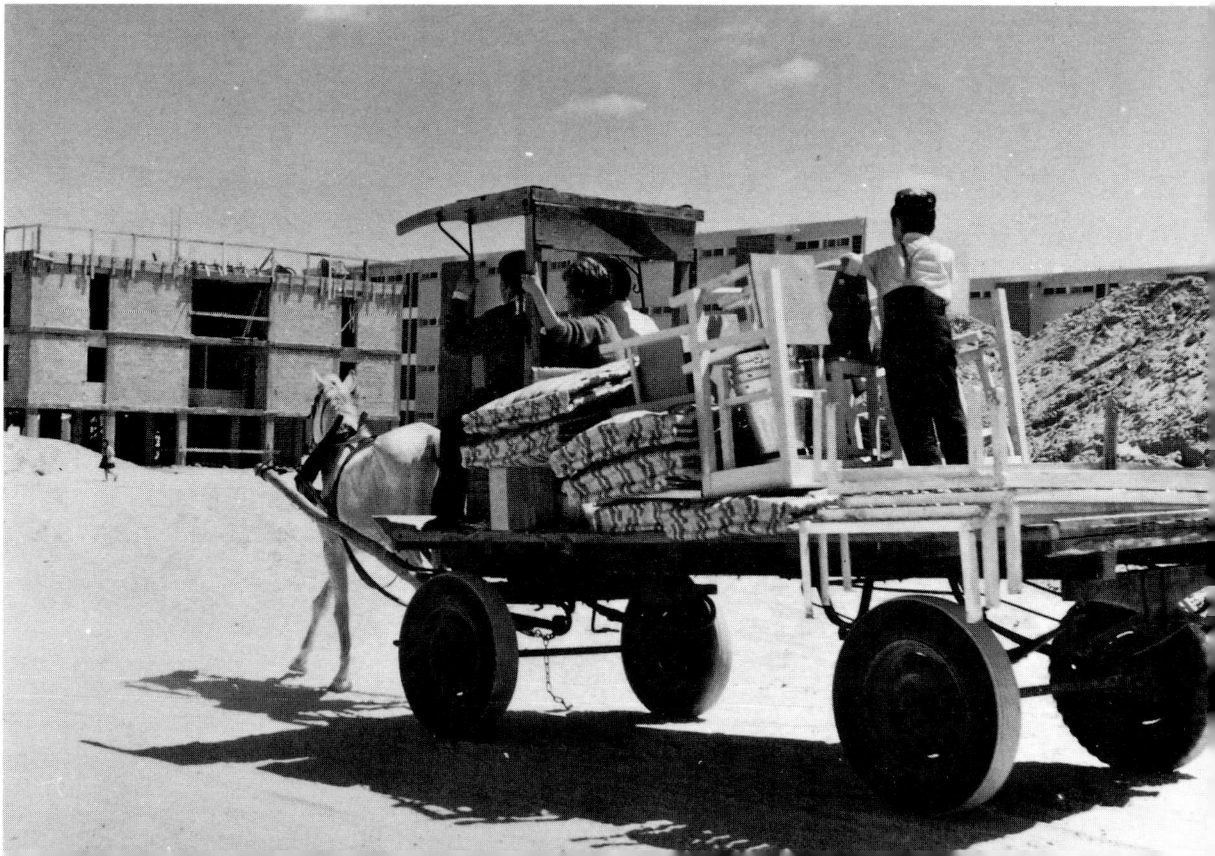

towns – and did remain unlovely landmarks until eventually they made way for units of flats, so cramped and so close together that these, too, contained the seeds of slumhood. There had not been time for proper investigation, for the application to the Ingathering of sound sociological research, for anthropologists to join architects over blueprints of immigrant housing. So mistakes were made and compounded; frictions and tensions added to hardships. Difficulties in communicating beset not only newcomers among themselves, but also sometimes gave rise to misunderstandings and resentment between immigrants and veteran settlers, between those who had to be taught to read and write, often how to use flush toilets, and their overworked, overwhelmed teachers.

But the network of services widened, new projects were launched, huge programmes of public works absorbed more and more newcomers – and conditions improved. Later, when immigrants from North Africa, Tunisia and Morocco began to arrive at the rate of 5,000 a month, new rules and better procedures were used: no more sprawling impersonal reception centres, no more drifting to cities where adequate accommodation and/or work could not be found; more independence, right from Day One; medical and other screening carried out, whenever feasible, at the place of origin and questions asked which would make it possible for newcomers to be taken straight from airfield or port to homes which, potentially at least, were permanent – or to farms where they found also small inventories of poultry or livestock, eager instructors and quotas of workdays to tide them over till their farms yielded income. These methods too were not problem-free or error-proof but 'Operation Ship to Settlement' was positively streamlined compared with earlier arrangements; and although each wave of immigration – whether it was Polish and Hungarian Jews in the middle 1950s, Soviet Jews in the 1970s or Ethiopian Jews in the 1980s – gave rise, perhaps unavoidably, to a certain amount of protest, discontent and self-criticism, by 1961 Israel had absorbed 1,017,153 immigrants.

The years 1948 and 1949 were those in which everything had to be done very quickly or it might not get done at all. Israel's Provisional Government, which had directed the war, levied the nation's first taxes and set up the first essential administrative agencies, now had to become a regular government. In January 1949, national elections were held (86 per cent of the population participating) to fill 120 seats of a unicameral parliament, the Knesset, which took its name and number of seats from the Great Assembly, the Jewish

51 Israel's first Cabinet, installed in March 1949, included Golda Meir as Minister of Labour, Moshe Sharett as Foreign Minister and Zalman Shazar as Minister of Education and Culture.

52 Chaim Weizmann takes the oath as Israel's first President, February 1949. On his right, Joseph Sprinzak, Knesset Speaker.

representative body convened in the fifth century BC. In February 1949, the Knesset (which included three Arab members) inaugurated a permanent government, installed Israel's first President, and its first Prime Minister, David Ben-Gurion. It held its initial session in a hastily refurbished Tel Aviv cinema and then moved to Jerusalem into a building originally intended as a bank, only settling in its striking permanent home (donated by James de Rothschild) in 1966. The most important ordinance it enacted (in July 1950) was the Law of the Return, giving legal force to the pledge contained in the Proclamation of Independence which declared the inalienable right of every Jew to settle in the Land and, by so doing, to acquire Israeli nationality. The choice of President, like that of Prime Minister, was obvious; Dr Chaim Weizmann's right to the honour was unquestioned. Aging and half-blind, he died in 1952 and was buried in the lovely garden of his house, overlooking the campus of the Weizmann Institute.

The siege had caused the new state's headquarters to be located in Tel Aviv rather than Jerusalem (though Israel's Supreme Court, from the beginning, sat in David's City), but it was clear that Chaim Weizmann's induction and the first Knesset session could be held nowhere else. By 1950, after the UN General Assembly once again stated its intention to internationalize Jerusalem, most Ministries – though not the Ministries of Defence or Foreign Affairs – moved there, to what, for a long time, were makeshift offices scattered through the city. At the UN, the Jerusalem question, with some regularity, bobbed to the surface and submerged; after a while, Israel's *de facto* guardianship of the Christian and Moslem holy places being beyond reproach, the pressures were reduced for changing its status. In the summer of 1953, the Foreign Ministry quietly packed papers and personnel and next day opened for business, as usual, in Jerusalem.

Not everyone accepted the *fait accompli*; some governments, led by the United States and Britain (though at the UN neither had voted in favour of internationalization), announced that their missions would not take the high road to Jerusalem and their staffs would not visit the Foreign Ministry; some even continued addressing communications to Tel Aviv. With time, hardline positions softened, but on any given day, Israelis can see the cars of the unreconciled driving up and down between Tel Aviv and the capital, since most embassies and legations are still not in Jerusalem. As for Israel's foreign service, in the first flush of statehood, its founders planned to do without embassies and to make the highest diplomatic rank that of minister; but when in January 1949 the US granted *de jure* recognition and, a month later,

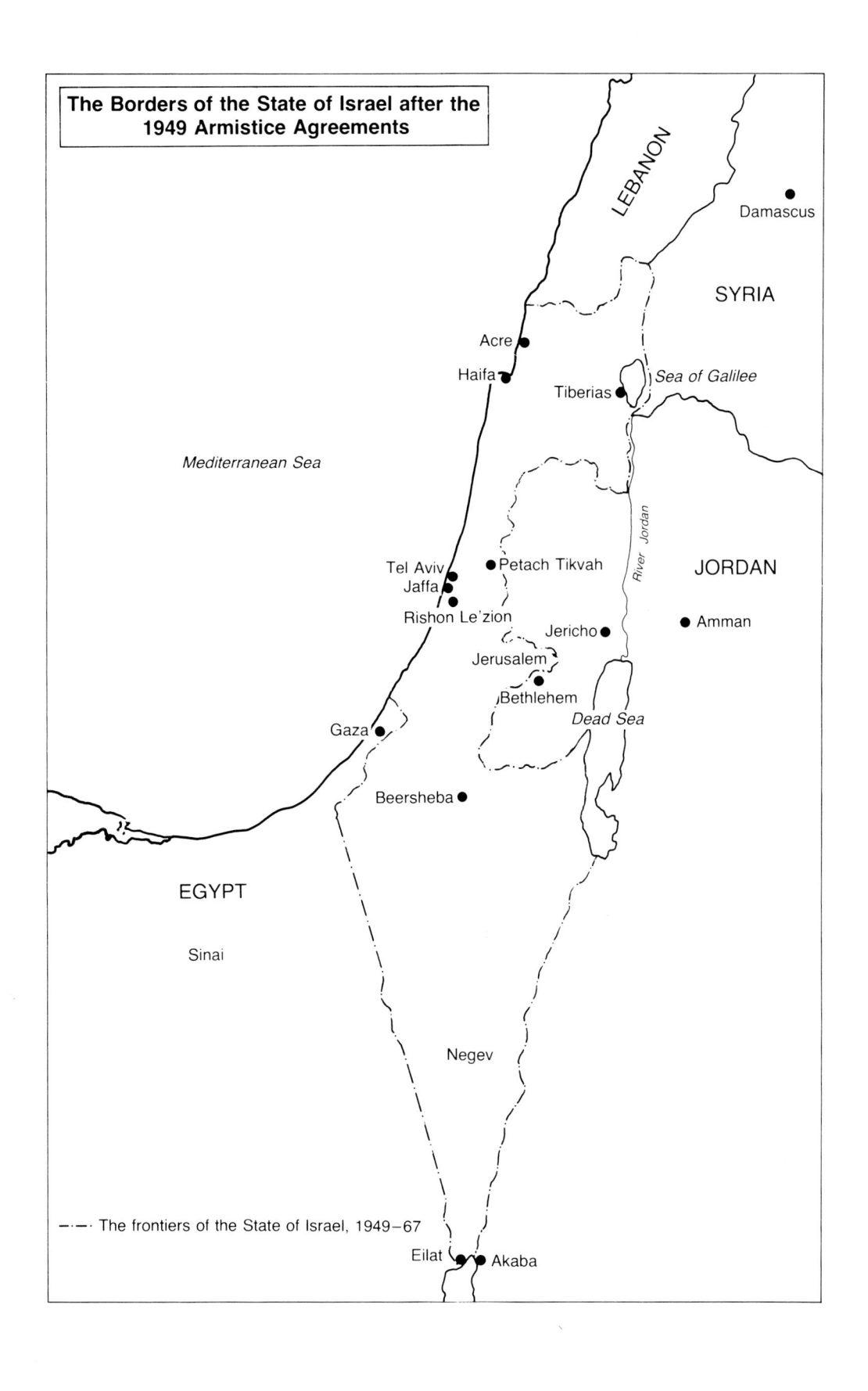

The Borders of the State of Israel after the 1949 Armistice Agreements

—·—· The frontiers of the State of Israel, 1949–67

appointed an ambassador, Israel happily reciprocated.

US recognition led the rest. In March 1948, Chaim Weizmann had been warmly received at the White House by President Truman; in May, following a surprise proposal — made at the UN by the head of the US delegation — to delay establishment of the state and introduce a temporary trusteeship, Weizmann wrote anxiously to Truman, expressing hope that the US would promptly recognize 'the new Jewish state'. Truman, much taken by Weizmann (to whom he referred affectionately as 'the old Doctor'), greatly appreciated Weizmann's views and his sombre assessment of the future of the Jews of Palestine if independence were to be postponed — and made a momentous decision. On 13 May, Weizmann was told that a formal request for recognition of the still-unborn state should be delivered to the White House; another letter went off at once. The response was split-second; at 5.15 p.m. on 14 May — without prior warning to the US team at the United Nations — President Truman authorized the *de facto* recognition by the US of what he had just been informed was to be called Israel, where the British mandate had just ended and the 'new Jewish state' had begun. 'American recognition came to the embattled Jews ... as an unexpected act of grace,' Abba Eban was to write. 'They were no longer forsaken or alone.' Next to follow the US example were Guatemala and, two days later, the Soviet Union.

'We waited two thousand years for a Jewish state and it had to happen to me!' was one of the sayings with which Israelis amused themselves in the exciting, trying and tiring years which followed the War of Independence. A great deal was being achieved: some 200 new settlements were founded in the course of the state's first eighteen months; thousands of acres of newly irrigated land were helping to fill the national bread-basket — at a time when severe austerity dictated that almost everything was strictly rationed (including clothing and shoes); Bibles in hand, teams of experts combed the state, especially the Negev, for minerals and found commercially useful copper, iron ore and manganese; the country hummed with the sounds of construction, exploration and social experimentation, but these mingled also with the sounds of hatred.

Once the armistice agreements were signed, the Arabs looked around for other means of continuing their war-to-the-end against Israel, and found some. The Arab boycott touched upon many critical areas of Israel's economic life; a 'black list' was compiled of all ships known to call at Israeli ports, of all companies that traded with Israel or maintained branches there; regulations

53 Israel becomes the fifty-ninth member of the United Nations while Abba Eban (third left) and Moshe Sharett (far right) watch the blue-and-white Israeli flag rise at the then UN headquarters at Flushing Meadows, New York, May 1949.

enacted by the Arab states prohibited aircraft from flying over their territory on their way to or from the Jewish state, while travel eastwards from Israel was made impossible, and visas to these states were refused to anyone whose passport contained a visa for Israel, so tourists who wanted also to visit Jordan or Egypt, for instance, had to equip themselves with two passports. The boycott, of course, incorporated the blockade of the Suez Canal through which no Israeli ship could pass for years, and that of the Gulf of Akaba, where, at the tip of the Sinai Peninsula, Egyptian guns guaranteed that not a single vessel could call at Israel's new port of Eilat. It was not so much these measures (which, as was subsequently proved, could have been rendered ineffectual by international refusal to tolerate them) that depressed the Israelis; it was knowing that, as far as the Arabs were concerned, the war was an on-going multi-faceted process with which, like it or not, they would have to deal for a very long time.

CHAPTER 6

The First Decade

Given its complexity, its difficult geopolitical position, the multiplicity and obstinacy of its foes, it was inevitable that Israel's first decade – and, as a matter of fact, all those that have followed – was accompanied by virtually incessant crises. In some instances, the crucial issues facing the young state were political and military, thus belonging to the category of predictable if urgent problems which beset most nations at one time or another, and can be, and are, dealt with by action – however temporary its effect. But there were also major domestic confrontations on topics unique to Israel, inherently Israeli, even perhaps inseparable from the very existence, in the twentieth century, of a Jewish state, which, because they stemmed from the totality of the Jewish experience, have, in fact, not yet disappeared from the national agenda – and, indeed, may never do so. The need – in both cases – to arrive quickly at the most satisfactory (i.e. the safest), least traumatic decisions possible characterized the considerable intellectual, emotional and tactical challenges facing Israelis in the 1950s.

'The State of Israel will be open for Jewish immigration and for the Ingathering of Exiles' – so declared the Proclamation of Independence. The Law of the Return, passed in July 1950, gave legal sanction to the fundamental principle that every Jew was entitled to settle in the Land and to receive free, and automatic, citizenship, something accorded also to every Jew who had settled there before the Law was passed and to all Jews born in the country, either before or after that. This secular Law, dryly expressing the essence of Zionism, opened the way to a continuing search for a definition – acceptable to most Israeli Jews – that would adequately answer the now entirely practical question: who is a Jew? It led also to the exacerbation of long-standing tensions between the stricter elements of the Orthodox establishment and the non-religiously observant majority, a conflict rooted in the obvious and ever-growing need for the co-existence of highly divergent beliefs regarding the proper place of Judaism within the Jewish state.

Because the Orthodox establishment was represented in Israel's political life – as in the Zionist movement – by a number of active, strongly motivated clerical parties (often holding the balance of power in Israel's traditional coalition governments), the influence and impact of rabbinical law and its interpretation was, and is, substantial – even though Israel is a secular democracy. For the sake of stability, in order to avoid, or at least postpone, a most hurtful, possibly fruitless showdown, compromise has been the order of the day. Rather than cope with fundamentalist assertions that the Torah was, in fact, Israel's constitution and no other required, Israel has managed without a written constitution; although there is no official state religion, a Ministry of Religious Affairs cares for the religious needs of *all* communities (including the Moslem Arabs who make up some 77 per cent of Israel's over 710,000 non-Jews, the Christians – mostly Arabs – who account for 13.5 per cent of this population, and the 9.5 per cent Druze, followers of a sect that split from Islam in the eleventh century); a widespread state religious educational network – from kindergarten to *yeshivot* (centres for higher instruction in Jewish learning) – is maintained and rabbinical courts as in mandatory times hold sway over matters of Jewish personal status (marriage, divorce, alimony, etc.).

The increasing prevalence of private cars, the troubleshooting talents of many Israeli personalities, the public's innate appreciation of the Jewish tradition of Sabbath serenity, have all tended to limit what might otherwise have developed into intolerable friction over the issue of Sabbath observance – though sporadic and unpleasant outbreaks of anti-secularism have not been totally prevented. This, notwithstanding the enforced absence over the Israeli weekend (all told, a day and a half) of public transportation, any newspapers and open places of amusement. Of course, maintenance of life and security are always overriding.

Not all such restrictions have been bearable; from time to time, individual distress has resulted in appeals being brought to the civil courts against rulings, based on religious law, particularly where Jewish identity, for whatever reason, is in question.

In the 1950s, one such case was triggered by the application for Israeli citizenship, under the Law of the Return, by a Carmelite monk, Brother Daniel, a.k.a. Oswald Rufeisen. He was no ordinary monk. A Polish Jew who had helped to save other Jews from the Holocaust, he had himself been saved by Catholics – after which he had converted, become a monk, and arrived in Israel to join the community of the Carmelite Monastery, named for, and located on, Mount Carmel. When he applied for citizenship through regular channels, the Ministry of the Interior explained that Brother Daniel could certainly become naturalized but should not expect to be recognized as Jewish for the purpose of instant citizenship. His argument that he was a Jewish national of the Catholic religion was not accepted. The State Attorney, quoting Herzl, UNSCOP and the Talmud among others, summed up by saying: 'It is not enough for the applicant to say that he feels Jewish. Jewishness is not a fraternity based on mere feeling.' Brother Daniel persisted and eventually the case came before the Supreme Court sitting as the High Court of Justice. There the paradox was revealed, and upheld: according to religious law, Brother Daniel did not cease to be a Jew because he converted to another religion; a born Jew remains Jewish regardless of any procedures undertaken to erase this inborn attribute. However, four of the five judges agreed that a professing Christian could not possibly be considered Jewish. One Justice wrote:

> If I could follow the dictates of my heart, I would allow the petitioner's prayer. But, to my regret I am duty-bound to interpret the term 'Jew' in the Law of the Return, as it is understood in our days in the parlance of the people.... The petitioner has ... consistently ... and in the best of faith proclaimed that he is a Jew by race, taking pride in his Jewishness, which was forged by such suffering and courage.... Howsoever anomalous the position may be ... the Jewish people as such have always regarded a fellow Jew who became an apostate as having abandoned not only his religion but his race ... it is in this spirit that the Law of the Return was framed.

Brother Daniel remained in Israel, was naturalized in 1963 and gladly vanished from the headlines he had occupied for quite a while until 1976, when, on the occasion of the hijacking of an Air France jet liner to Entebbe, he offered to go to Uganda in exchange for one of the Israeli hostages.

Another convoluted, though more painful, issue concerned the Holocaust and focused on guilt: the irrational guilt of those who had survived; the guilt induced by the possibility that the Zionist movement had not done enough to bring the state into being earlier so that it might, perhaps, have availed the Jews of Europe; and the guilt of those Jews who had actually dealt with the Nazis — on their own behalf or that of others. One agonizing example of the latter was a singularly grim sequence of events which started in the Budapest offices of the ss in March 1944 and ended a decade later with shots fired one night on a pleasant Tel Aviv street. In the spring of 1944, the Nazis invaded Hungary, their presence dooming some 800,000 Hungarian Jews to eventual death in Nazi extermination centres. In the dire emergency, Dr Rudolf Kastner, a worldly and talented Jewish journalist who then functioned as Deputy Chairman of the Hungarian Zionist Organization, headed up a small, secret and desperate team that attempted to persuade German intelligence officers to trade the lives of Jews for money.

The negotiations were intense and terrible; in the end, no longer certain of victory, the Nazis made their notorious 'Blood for Goods' proposal in which, via neutral countries, supplies financed by Jewish organizations in the West would be received for the German war effort in exchange for the survival of the Jewish population and its transfer abroad from German-occupied territories. In connection with this rescue plan, Kastner visited Germany several times in 1944 and 1945 and, in the summer of 1944, managed to get the Nazis to permit two transports, totalling 1,866 prominent Hungarian Jews, including his own family and friends, to leave for Switzerland, from where most of them found their way to the Land. After the war, Kastner testified at the Nuremberg trials in favour of three Nazi officers, thus helping to save their lives. Eventually, he settled in Tel Aviv, became a spokesman for the Ministry of Tourism and Industry, a Labour Party candidate for the Knesset and editor of a Hungarian daily newspaper.

In 1954, a seventy-two-year-old Orthodox Jew, Malkiel Greenwald, wrote and published a mimeographed leaflet in which he accused Kastner of co-operating with the Nazis, Adolf Eichmann among them, and therefore collaborating in the annihilation of Hungarian Jewry. Since Kastner worked for the Government, the Attorney-General instituted a libel case against Greenwald. At the trial, however, Greenwald's accusations were upheld. 'Kastner has sold his soul to the devil,' declared the District Court Judge, dismissing the case. The arguments for and against Kastner's culpability turned into a major source of partisan rancour in Israel's 1955 elections; the ferocious public campaign waged against him ended in Kastner's murder by a young assailant in 1957. A year later, the Supreme Court reversed the original verdict, posthumously clearing Kastner's name. The trial, the reopening of still-unhealed wounds, the drama of vengeance, recrimination and despair, shook Israel deeply. Nor has the Kastner case faded from view,

54 Orthodox Jewry in Israel is multi-faceted including the many moderate believers who wear contemporary dress, do army service and form an integral part of Israeli society – and the twentieth century.

55 Ultra-Orthodox Jews have, for years, clashed with police over a Jerusalem excavation which, they claim, disturbs ancient graves in sharp violation of Jewish law.

despite the decades. As recently as 1987, under extreme public pressure, a leading London theatre withdrew from its boards a play, *Perdition*, based on the Kastner story, and a new book on the subject came out in Israel.

Another altogether different exploration that flowered in the 1950s, engaging the intelligence, imagination and seemingly limitless energies of thousands upon thousands of Israelis was archaeology: part relaxation, part hobby, but in the main a widely shared passion for investigating, illuminating and verifying what had taken place in the distant past of the Land. Modern excavations of Palestine were under way long before the establishment of the state: the first was made in 1850 by a French explorer; the earliest scientific work dated from 1865 and the foundation of the American Palestine Exploration Fund, both motivated largely to prove the Bible true. But for Israelis, the 'digs' meant something additional, more than the chance to learn about antiquity: archaeology unfolded for them their own origins, as it were, and enabled them to extrapolate from newly acquired information whatever might enrich the present; for instance, exactly where in the Land large populations had once settled and prospered, as, it turned out, they had done in various parts of the Negev. Archaeology riveted public attention; lectures, books, archaeological conventions, sites and, of course, on-going work were, and are, in the news, often making headlines, constantly absorbing topics of general conversation.

Among the most famous modern archaeological finds are the Dead Sea Scrolls, dating back to the first century BC, which include complete Hebrew manuscripts of the Book of Isaiah, an apocalyptic poem about the struggle between the Sons of Light and the Sons of Darkness, and fragments of almost every book of the Hebrew Bible. The first seven scrolls were found in a cave at the north-west of the Dead Sea in 1947; many more were discovered in 1951, among them letters written by Bar-Kochba at the time of the rebellion he led against Rome from 132 to 135 AD. Written in the first person singular, apparently dictated to different people, more like memos than missives, and composed, it seems, by a heartsick commander in the last days of a failing struggle, the letters (part of a rich trove of possessions: textiles, mats, baskets, bronze, etc.) waste no words on niceties. Probably about a shirker, Bar-Kochba writes: 'send him to me in safe custody ... and do not neglect to take off his sword'; about reinforcements: 'get hold of the young men ... and come with them; if not – a punishment ... I shall deal with the Romans'; about supplies: 'send to the camp four loads of salt'.

Equally gripping, perhaps largest of all the archaeological endeavours attempted thus far in the Land, was the excavation of Masada, Herod's rock fortress hundreds of feet above the Dead Sea, built around 37 BC as a haven against attack by Cleopatra, and serving, in 73 AD, as the last centre of Jewish resistance to Rome. One of the first archaeological undertakings following the establishment of the state was a trial excavation of the buildings on the mountain, carried out in 1955–6 by a joint effort of the Government, the Israel Defence Forces, the Hebrew University and the Israel Exploration Society. In time, all the structures were cleared, some reconstructed and a wealth of finds collected, ranging from cooking utensils and coins (inscribed 'For the Freedom of Zion') to priceless biblical scrolls that included parts of the Book of Genesis, Leviticus, Deuteronomy, Psalms and Ezekiel. Like the Dead Sea Scrolls, they were written in the same Hebrew that is in contemporary usage, and in text and spelling are identical with the Bible.

The moving spirit behind both the Masada and Bar-Kochba excavations was Professor Yigael Yadin, credited in 1949, as Israel's young second Chief of Staff, with establishing the standing army, compulsory military service and the IDF system of reserves. His best-selling books about his expeditions simultaneously symbolized, and fed, Israel's consuming curiosity as to how it had really been all those millennia ago.

Within the country, new contents, ancient contexts, all manner of continuities and conclusions were being examined, but as always – so it already seemed after less than ten years of independence – the true test of the strength of the national fabric was being forced upon Israel from outside. The infiltration of armed Arab gangs across Israel's frontiers had begun, even before the armistice agreements were signed. At first, it was assumed that these were 'unprofessional' raids, aimed at filching crops and cattle from Jewish border settlements. All too soon, however, murder accompanied the marauding. By 1952, over 3,000 such incursions had taken place, leaving victims dead on mined roads, orange groves booby-trapped, fields burnt and homes destroyed, and, as the killings escalated, it became apparent that they were, mostly, being organized in Jordan and in Gaza on territory held by Egypt and supposedly demilitarized. In 1953, the Israel Defence Forces created a small tough unit, commanded by twenty-five-year-old Ariel Sharon, which was designed expressly for the purpose of hitting back, of reaching into and punishing Jordanian Arab Legion camps, Egyptian positions and whatever Syrian emplacements were also involved in the rising wave of terrorism. In

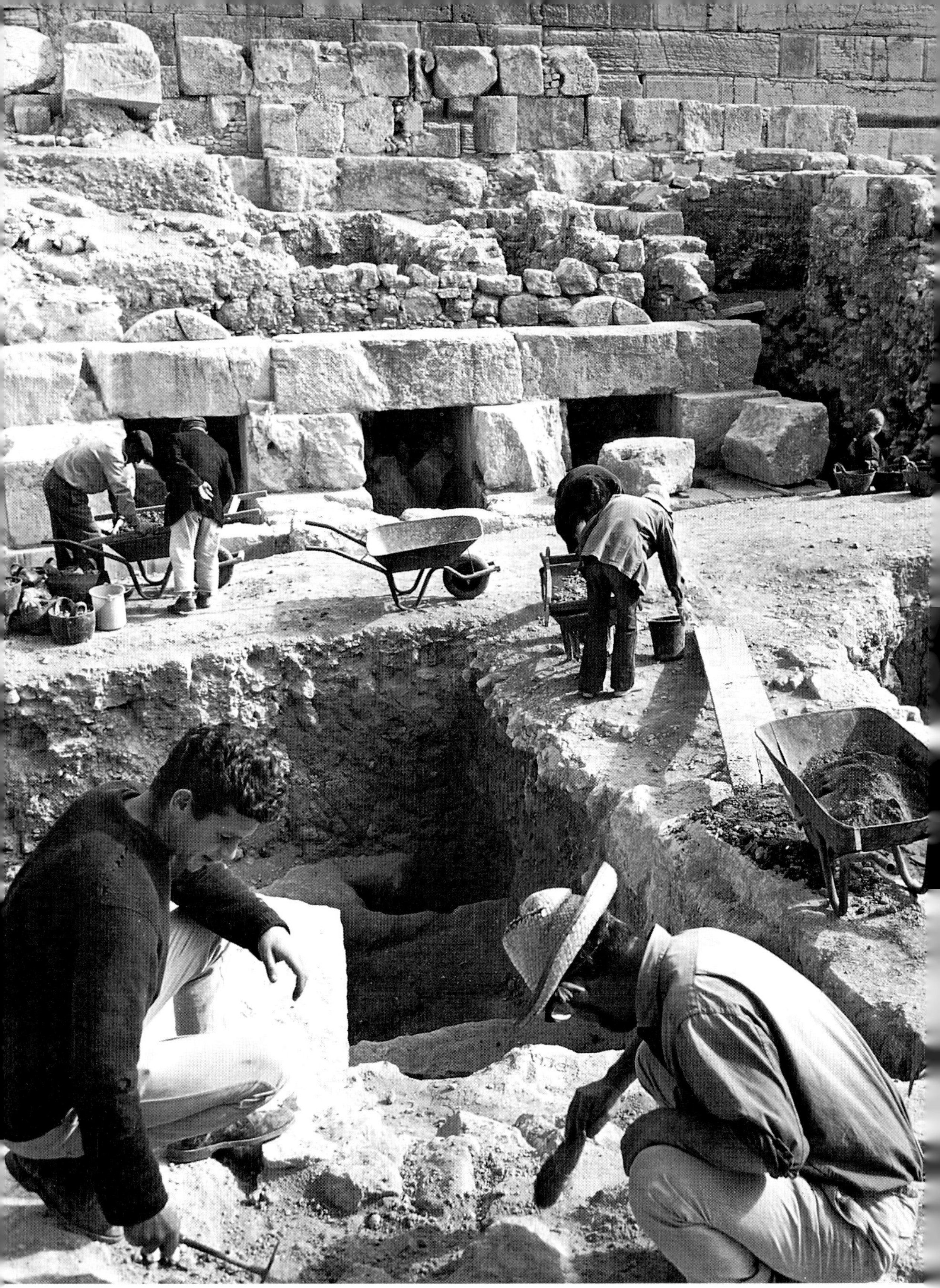

56 Opposite: Among the most interesting of Israel's 3,500 registered archaeological sites is the dig carried out in Jerusalem at the Western Wall.

57 Above: Professor Yigael Yadin examining one of the Dead Sea Scrolls.

the meanwhile, Israelis assured each other that, once again, there was no acceptable alternative to carrying on and went about their business, though not without trepidation, as the death toll mounted and the total number of actions carried out by the so-called *fedayeen* ('self-sacrificers') neared 12,000.

In 1954, Moshe Dayan became Israel's Chief of Staff. Backed by Prime Minister Ben-Gurion, he embarked on an aggressive security policy. 'We cannot,' he declared, 'save each water pipe from explosion or tree from being uprooted. We cannot prevent the murder ... of families in their beds. But we can put a very high price on their blood ... so high that it will no longer be worth while for the Arabs ... to pay it.'

By the end of summer 1955, there seemed no way to break the pattern of action and counter-action, of Arab terror and Israeli response, deadly volleying which only just skirted being open warfare. Israeli anger was reinforced by continuation of the illegal blockade against the passage of Israeli shipping through the Suez Canal and the Straits of Tiran. An Israeli vessel, the *Bat-Galim*, was sent to and reached the southern approaches to the Canal, it being thought that if Egypt refused to let her through, the UN would at last be obliged to consider the issue seriously. The Egyptians at once seized the ship, imprisoned her crew and continued to ignore international law while the UN continued to do nothing. As large-scale retaliatory actions replaced earlier guerrilla tactics, civilian casualties dropped, but military casualties rose. Dayan helped to remind Israelis that, in the interests of national security, they would have to overcome their sensitivity to losses. 'Let us not be afraid', he declared in May 1956, at the funeral of a young kibbutznik tortured to death near the Gaza Strip, 'to see the enmity that consumes the lives of hundreds of thousands of Arabs around us. Let us not avert our gaze for it will weaken our hand. This is the fate of our generation. The only choice we have is to be armed, strong and resolute....'

In the background lurked the Soviet Union. A so-called Czech arms deal, concluded in 1955 with the Government of Egypt, which lavished weapons not only on the *fedayeen* but also on the Egyptian army, instantly upset the shaky arms balance between the Arab states and Israel and gave Egypt a four-fold advantage in tanks and warplanes. The President of Egypt, Gamal Abdel Nasser, publicly clarified whatever might still be obscure; he promised the Egyptian people that they would 'reconquer' Palestine, and promptly translated promise into deed. That summer he seized and nationalized the

Suez Canal – for a hundred years controlled by the British Government and French investors – thus ensuring that not only Israel but also the rest of the world would appreciate his position as the outstanding leader of the Arabs.

In October, Nasser strode further down the war-path: the Egyptian, Syrian and Jordanian high commands were unified under an Egyptian Supreme Commander, their troops, armour and artillery concentrated in Sinai, and the blockade of the Gulf of Akaba intensified. Israel, glumly contemplating a rapidly worsening situation, was informed by the French and British that if it acted, it would not be alone; determined to obliterate Egyptian army and *fedayeen* bases in Sinai and Gaza and open the Red Sea to Israeli shipping, it set about reluctantly preparing for war again. This time, however, the Jewish state would choose the time and the place. The spectacular surprise assault in which, on 29 October 1956, a mortal blow was delivered by Israel to Nasser's strength and prestige – despite Egypt's superiority in arms, equipment and men – is known in Israel as 'Operation Kadesh' (for the biblical site where the Children of Israel probably organized for their attempt to penetrate the Land). Elsewhere, it was viewed as Act One of the still profoundly controversial Sinai Campaign of which Act Two was the Anglo-French 'Operation Musketeer', intended to retake the Canal from Nasser while the Egyptians were distracted by an Israeli onslaught.

The initiative for a collaborative military venture was French; it came at a time when France was the only power willing to provide Israel, albeit secretly, with arms and other military equipment and was therefore perceived by Israel as a provenly trustworthy friend. Britain, national pride badly stung by Nasser's blatant defiance, was, however, both less eager and less prepared for the proposed campaign, but none the less went along with the idea. As for Israel, Ben-Gurion – also not especially enthusiastic about the suggested collaboration – demanded, and was given, a number of iron-clad guarantees against the state's being left in the lurch by its putative partners. The scenario finally presented by the French, but turned down by Israel, was that the IDF would attack Egypt, following which the peacemaking French and British would be seen to put a firm stop to the fighting. In the end, Dayan persuaded the French and British that Israel would make its first strike near the Canal so that, if unsuccessful, the operation could be explained as a major push against the *fedayeen* in Sinai.

A *sine qua non* of 'Operation Kadesh' was absolute secrecy; the call-up began, almost imperceptibly, on 25 October and went on for four days. Routines, often rehearsed, paid off; within four days, nine Israeli brigades were ready for action. Late in the afternoon of 29 October, Israeli parachutists dropped in the heart of the Sinai Peninsula, at the Mitla Pass, less than forty miles from the Canal while two mobile columns pushed their way through trackless desert to join them. Another force opened the road to Eilat and, without pausing, dashed to link up with the parachute battalion at night. By the fourth day, the Israelis had travelled farther and faster in that unfamiliar and harsh terrain than any combat troops had done before, taking with them thousands of prisoners and massive military booty, most of it made in the USSR. One part of the IDF tore on towards the Canal; a second raced towards the Gaza Strip; a third forced its way 700 miles through the scorching sands of eastern Sinai to Sharm el-Sheikh.

By 5 November, 'Operation Kadesh' was over: all Sinai was in Israel's hands. The Egyptian defeat was total: the Egyptian army demoralized and in flight, 1,000 Egyptian soldiers dead, over 6,000 more taken prisoner. Israel mourned the 180 young men who had fallen in the war, worried about the wounded pilot brought down behind enemy lines and the four Israeli prisoners of war, but rejoiced that Kadesh had succeeded and prayed that it would be the last of Israel's wars. But Kadesh was the only success of the Sinai Campaign, and a short-lived one at that. The partners had done badly; on 30 October, an ultimatum, that original carefully worked-out pretext, was issued to the Israelis and Egyptians by the Anglo-French 'peacemakers', demanding that both sides at once vacate the Canal area. As the scenario had anticipated, neither side paid heed to the warning, so on 31 October, the peacemakers bombarded Egypt from the air and, at week's end, entered Port Said.

Abroad, pandemonium broke out. The UN met in all-night emergency session, its outcome a condemnation of the Anglo-French conspiracy and of Israel. The spokesmen of most of the nations of the world told everyone involved to clear out of Egypt at once and ordered the Israelis to retreat.

The US and the USSR, at each other's throats over the concurrent Soviet invasion of Hungary (which the partners had hoped would be an additional distraction), none the less pulled themselves together enough to unite against the trio and thus express a measure of support for the newly martyred Egyptian dictator – whose people, it should be noted, still knew nothing about what had befallen them in the desert.

The French and the British emerged from the Suez war in disarray and disgrace; Britain, divided and humiliated, France panicky about Soviet threats hinting at the possible use of nuclear weapons against the aggressors. The

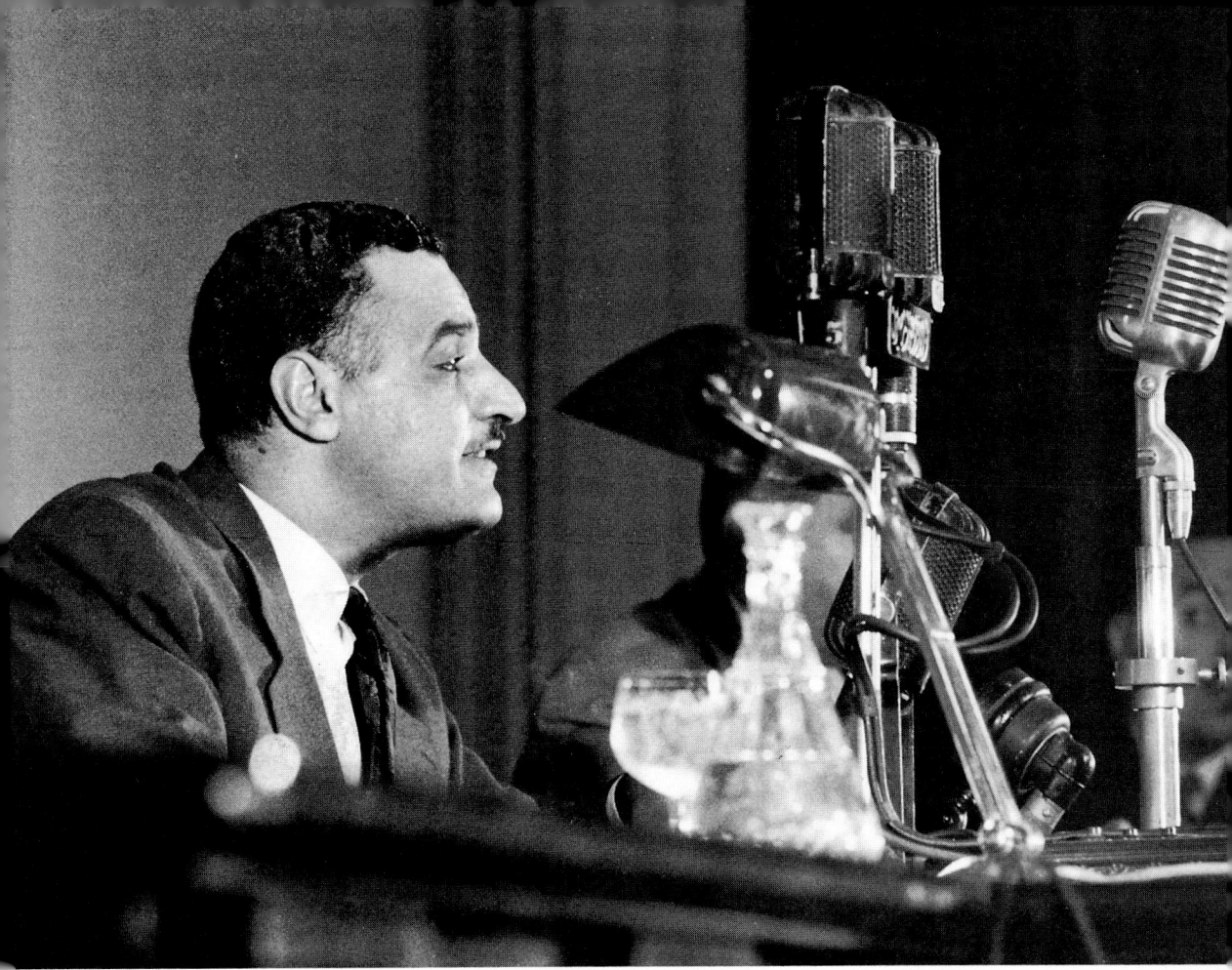

58 In 1956 Egyptian President, Gamal Abdel Nasser, the most powerful leader in the Arab world, saw Israel's destruction as vital to his vision of Egypt's future in the Middle East.

59 Prime Minister Ben-Gurion, Foreign Minister Sharett and British Foreign Secretary Selwyn Lloyd confer prior to the Sinai Campaign.

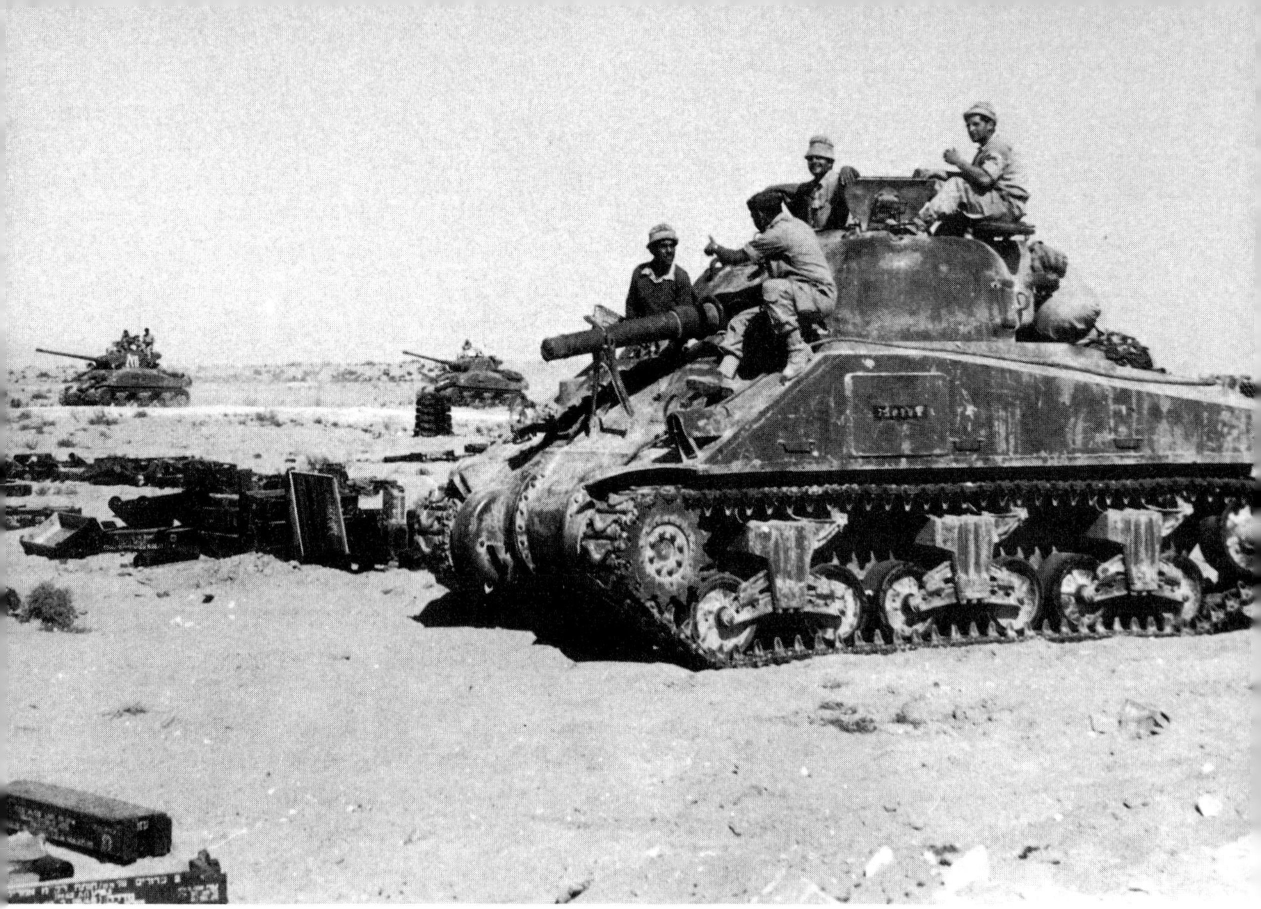

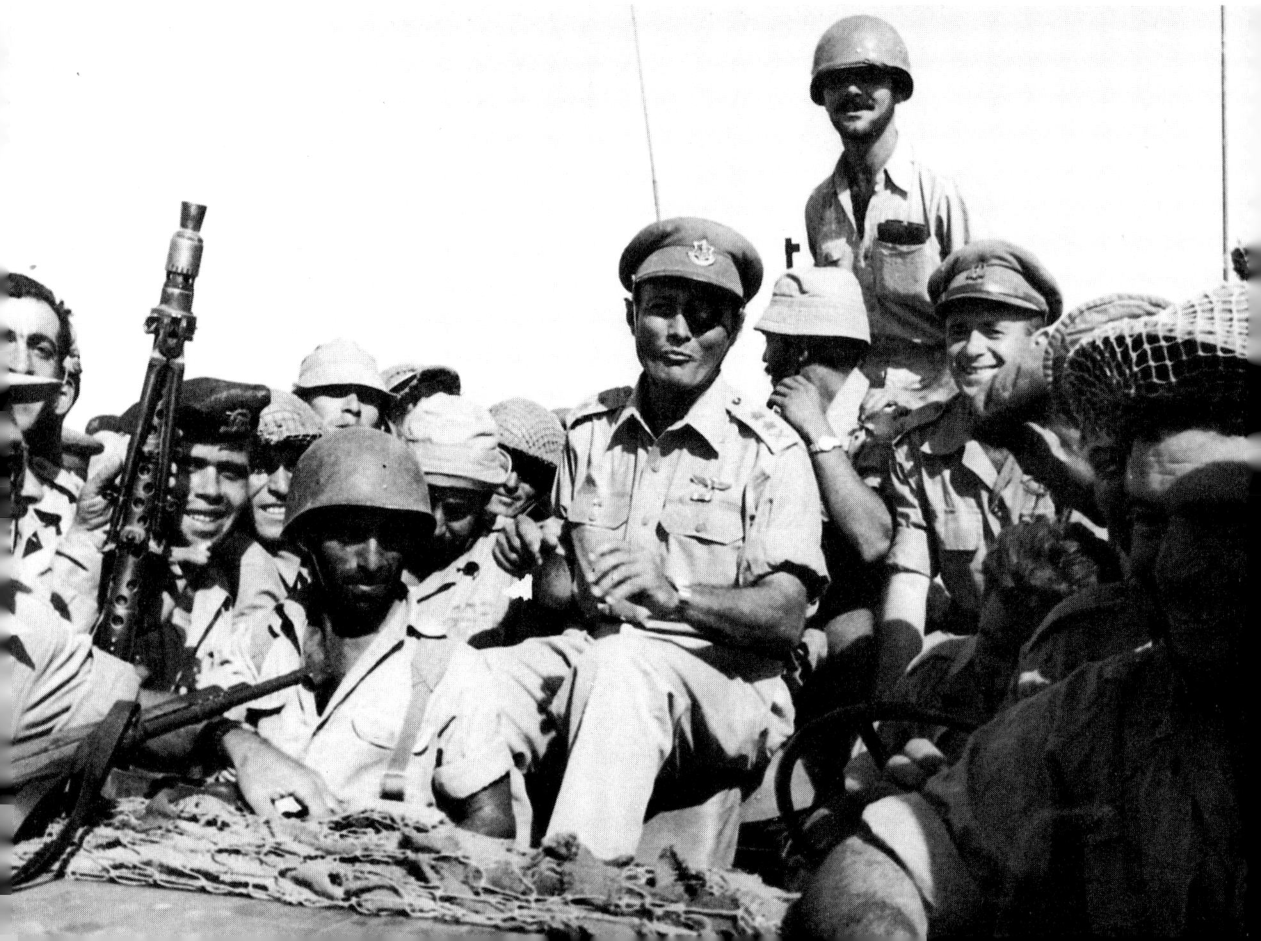

60 Opposite top: Israel had not fought Operation Kadesh for territory, prisoners or spoils, but the quantity of booty was overwhelming.

61 Opposite below: Moshe Dayan served as IDF Chief of Staff from 1953 to 1958 and commanded Israeli forces in Kadesh. On his left, Yitzhak Rabin, later to be Israel's Chief of Staff in 1967 and Prime Minister in 1974.

62 Above: The IDF withdrawing from the Sinai Peninsula – for the first time, December 1956. At the very least there was hope for peace.

climate was hardly propitious for realization of Israel's war aims, but holding on to Sinai was the only guarantee for future peace and Israel tried hard, though to no avail, to stay put until peace talks and bargaining might begin. The diplomatic battle waged — and lost — by Israel at the UN took longer than the hundred hours of 'Operation Kadesh'; nearly five months were invested in trying to persuade the United Nations, but most especially the US and USSR, that no good could come of a withdrawal to the armistice lines of 1949, because war would only flare up again in the Middle East. But no one accepted the Israeli arguments, least of all US President Eisenhower and Soviet Prime Minister Nikolai Bulganin.

Heavy-hearted, apprehensive, sensing itself betrayed by the very body that had brought the state into existence, by the end of February 1957 Israel bitterly agreed to evacuate Sinai, the Gaza Strip and Sharm el-Sheikh in return for an 'assumption' that the UN would guarantee the right of free passage for Israeli shipping through the Straits of Tiran, that Egyptian soldiers would not be allowed back in the Gaza Strip, and that a UN Emergency Force would police the Israeli–Egyptian frontiers. In March 1957, the last Israeli troops left the Peninsula, their laurels fairly won, if grudgingly given and wilting a bit, hoping — though no historical logic dictated this optimism — that they would not have to fight in those sand dunes again.

CHAPTER 7

Confrontation and Achievement

The decade that followed the end of the Sinai Campaign, that witnessed the withdrawal of Israeli troops from the Sinai Peninsula, Sharm el-Sheikh and the Gaza Strip in the spring of 1957, and that drew to a close in 1967 with the outbreak of the Six Day War, did not, of course, bring Israel, aged nineteen, any nearer to real or lasting peace. But the terrorist bases had been destroyed, along with the twin myths of Arab unity and military skill; the UN (responsible for the state's birth) had re-entered the picture, certainly a good thing; Eilat could now breathe and develop; the borders were quiet. Not everything had been achieved, to put it mildly, but at least Israel could now go on with the job of consolidating existing gains and creating new ones. So growth became the imperative.

Economic expansion during the next few years was impressive; Israel's cities burst at the seams, producing quickly populated suburbs; the standard of living slowly rose; the average middle-class Israeli household at long last acquired a labour-saving appliance or two, and sometimes a car; and Israelis began to travel abroad, not only as emissaries. On a million or so cultivated acres, Israel was producing most of its own food. Also, life was developing in other important directions; research and scholarship flowered. Not everything was perfect; the rose garden – promised or otherwise – had its fair share of thorns. New immigrants, beginning to make their way in a bewildering, not always sensitive, society, frequently felt neglected and misunderstood, even though those accused of undervaluing the newcomers were the same men and women who had so often risked life and limb to bring them to Israel. Now, it was hard to remember that succour was still required, albeit in a different form. In the surge forward, other things were overlooked; aesthetics was one. For instance, the new housing that sprang up everywhere in response to the urgent need tended to be jerrybuilt, and looked it; old-timers watching

63 Industrial development in the 1960s. Here, a chemical plant takes profitable advantage of the nearby phosphate mines at Oron in the Negev.

64 Opposite: Israel's agricultural development was no less meteoric: the greening of the Kiryat Gat area associated with Goliath's birthplace and one of the five great Philistine cities ('Tell it not in Gath').

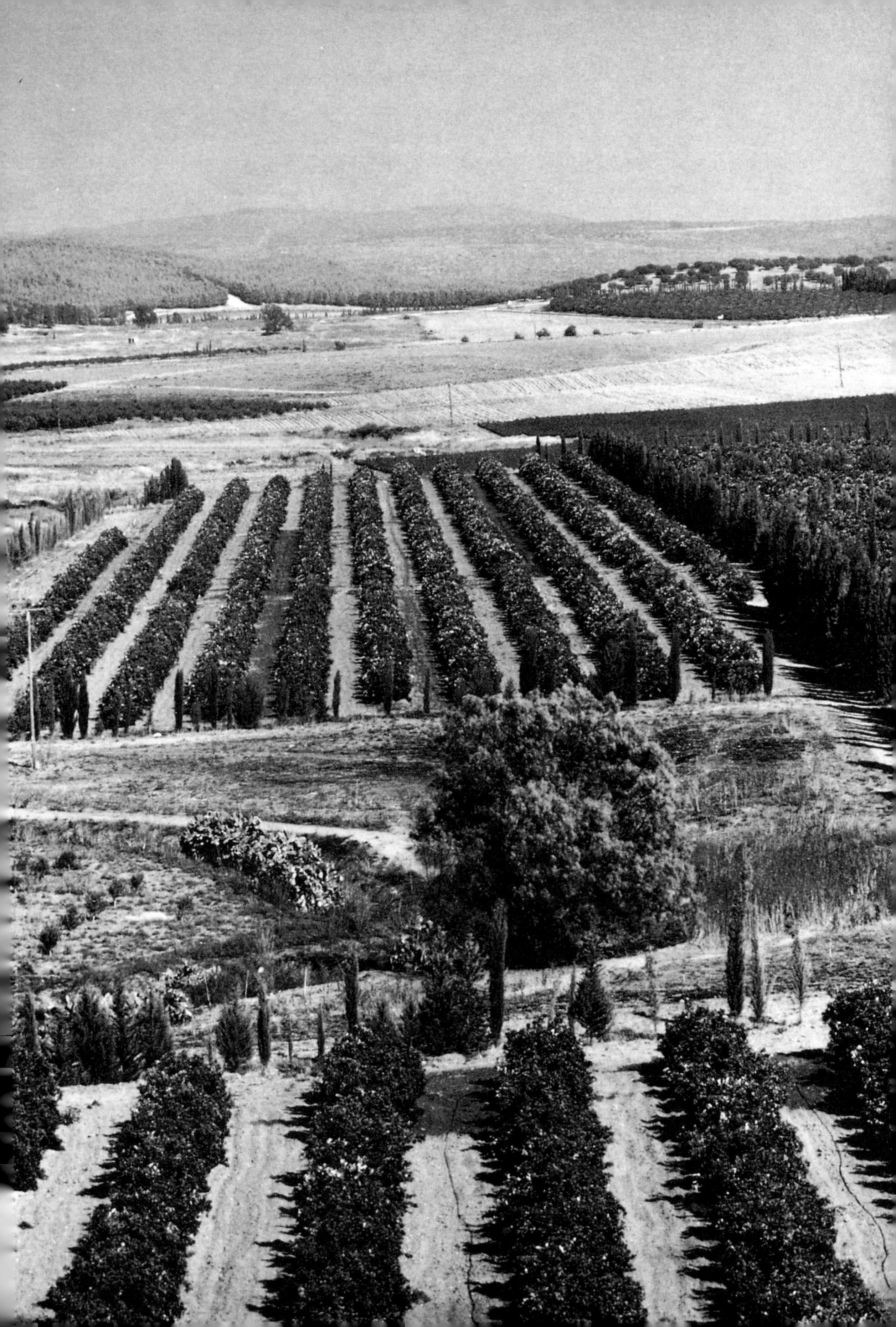

crowded housing estates turn into instant slums predicted that, even when tomorrow came, the ugly concrete blocks could never be bulldozed away, and condemned the newcomers for the billowing laundry, draped from each flat, that further added to unsightliness, forgetting that most immigrant families were large and that visible laundry was not, *a priori*, considered an eyesore. The tensions were many, various and mutual. Growing pains? Symptoms of troubles to come? Or merely melting-pot inevitabilities? Only time would tell.

A number of events both punctuated and typified the period, milestones indicating distances travelled thus far by the state. Against the background noises of would-be normality — earning a living, settling down in unfamiliar surroundings, or seeing to it that cultural integration was speeded up and enough jobs were found, with people trained to take and keep them — another note suddenly sounded, and everything around stilled.

At precisely 4 p.m., on 23 May 1960, speaking in the Knesset in Jerusalem, Prime Minister Ben-Gurion informed the nation that Karl Adolf Eichmann — who had helped organize the Nazi extermination programme as Director of Sub-Department IV W4b of the Reich Security Division SS — had been hunted down in Argentina and was now in Israel to stand trial under the 1950 Nazis and Nazi Collaborators Law. Ben-Gurion had not authorized Israel's vaunted intelligence service, Mossad, to find and capture Eichmann as a gesture to the past; his motives were infinitely weightier. It had long been felt in Israel that only inadequate steps had been taken to find and punish those responsible for the Nazi crimes of which thousands upon thousands of Israelis were the direct, grieving and maimed victims, and that although six million Jews had been murdered in Nazi death camps within the memory of every adult alive, the civilized world had somehow managed to avert its horrified gaze from the facts and their implications. Perhaps Ben-Gurion's gravest consideration was his conviction that Israel's youngsters, the country's children, must know the truth, learn what had happened, and be given the information by those who had endured the agony.

The trial opened in April 1961; it lasted for weeks and took a terrible toll. Day after day, ashen-faced witnesses related in detail what they themselves had experienced of the part played by Eichmann in the nightmare, while the rest of Israel sat riveted to radios; Eichmann, in his glass dock, listened with them to the awful testimonies, his expression never changing, his voice heard only when he gave the few essential answers required of him by law, and then he spoke only in monosyllables. Found guilty of crimes against humanity and against the Jewish people, and sentenced to death, his appeal to the Supreme Court turned down, he was hanged on 31 May 1962 in a small prison somewhere near Tel Aviv. His ashes were scattered at sea that night, the first (and so far, only) time that the death penalty was carried out under Israeli law. The trial had accomplished its primary aim: it had brought the lesson of the Holocaust home to all Israeli youth; children from Egypt, Yemen, Morocco and Iraq, for whom Hitler had never been much of a reality, now grasped the dimensions of the disaster that had befallen European Jewry — and this understanding too was part of the integration process.

Eichmann apart, the relationship between Israel and Germany was a constant preoccupation; a serious, potentially damaging rift in public opinion arose over the agreement, ratified in the autumn of 1959, for recompense of material damage caused by the Nazis to the Jews. 'The restoration as quickly as possible to individual Jews and to the Jewish people ... of the maximum amount of the plunder' was, as Ben-Gurion saw it, not only the fulfilling of a historic duty, but also something of pressing importance to the state's ability to survive economically — given the condition of the survivors of Nazism. The then German Chancellor Konrad Adenauer also saw this, and that Germany's post-World War II position might be substantially improved in this way. Neither leader was wrong; German funds alleviated the near-austerity of the immediate post-Sinai era; economic co-operation with Germany based largely on the investment of some $700 million (plus considerable personal restitution) yielded about $1 billion that went into building and development.

In addition to the passions unleashed by those who were appalled at dealing, in any way whatsoever, with Germany, there was one unforeseen and not trivial side-effect: Israel, initially so determinedly egalitarian, so solemnly accepting of the discomforts of pioneering, so given to the puritanism that tends to accompany Socialism, began to sprout *bona fide* 'haves' and 'have-nots'. German consumer goods were everywhere, available, however, only to a minority; hotels, resorts and restaurants sprang up under the impetus of the new thrust, but were only at the disposal of people who could afford them; those with no money at all, mostly new immigrants, did without the luxuries, felt ill-done-by and demanded more participation in everything. But Ben-Gurion was adamant, unswayed, though not unmoved, by the revulsion and bitter accusations that confronted him or by the outraged opposition to the reparations agreement of leaders such as Menachem Begin.

Within a few years, the Germans felt there was need for a far more closely defined connection, i.e. for diplomatic relations, a step postponed mainly due to Arab objections. In 1965, the first German Ambassador to Israel presented credentials to Israel's President Zalman Shazar in Jerusalem. Golda Meir was then Israel's Foreign Minister. An advocate of taking German money for building the Jewish state, she nevertheless dreaded her first meeting with the new envoy. 'I thought', she wrote later, 'that it was a moment for truth.... "You have a most difficult task before you," I said to him. "You cannot expect a warm reception. Even the women who will wait at table, if you ever come to me for a meal, have Nazi numbers tattooed on their arms".'

Twenty years after that grim welcome, the Holocaust is no longer at the centre of Israeli life but it is still inseparable from it. Yad Vashem is the national memorial to the six million, its name deriving from a verse in Isaiah in which God declares that He Himself will give to the unfortunate ' in mine house ... a place ... and an everlasting name that shall not be cut off'. Among those who have visited Yad Vashem and read these words are not only Chancellors Adenauer, Erhard, Kohl and Brandt, but also the President of the Federal German Republic Richard von Weizsäcker – whose son had been a summer student at Israel's noted Weizmann Institute of Science – and every single school child in the Land. Israeli sensitivities remain acute; the way German schools interpret the Holocaust – when they teach it at all, what the average German thinks and says about it, Germany's relations with the Arab states – are all subject to special scrutiny. But behaviour differs; some people refuse to visit Germany, do not permit the Israel Philharmonic to play Wagner or Strauss, buy nothing that is German; others choose to live more pragmatically, knowing that the tormented dead cannot be brought to life, and are willing to accept German penitence whenever it is expressed, and for what it is worth.

There was also the fulfilment – the mission and its accomplishments – that came to Israel in the 1960s from an entirely different direction, the unique flavour of which still lingers for many: the deep involvement of the state, through cadres of her best and brightest – agricultural instructors, teachers, doctors, nurses, experts in nutrition and in the organization of youth and community activities – in the development and well-being of the emerging states of Africa, Asia and many parts of Latin America. Wherever, in fact, Israeli know-how, enthusiasm and empathy were invited and could be usefully

65 Adolf Eichmann on trial, Jerusalem 1961.

66 Touring a permanent exhibition at Yad Vashem, young Israelis begin to absorb the ghastly truth of the Nazi Holocaust.

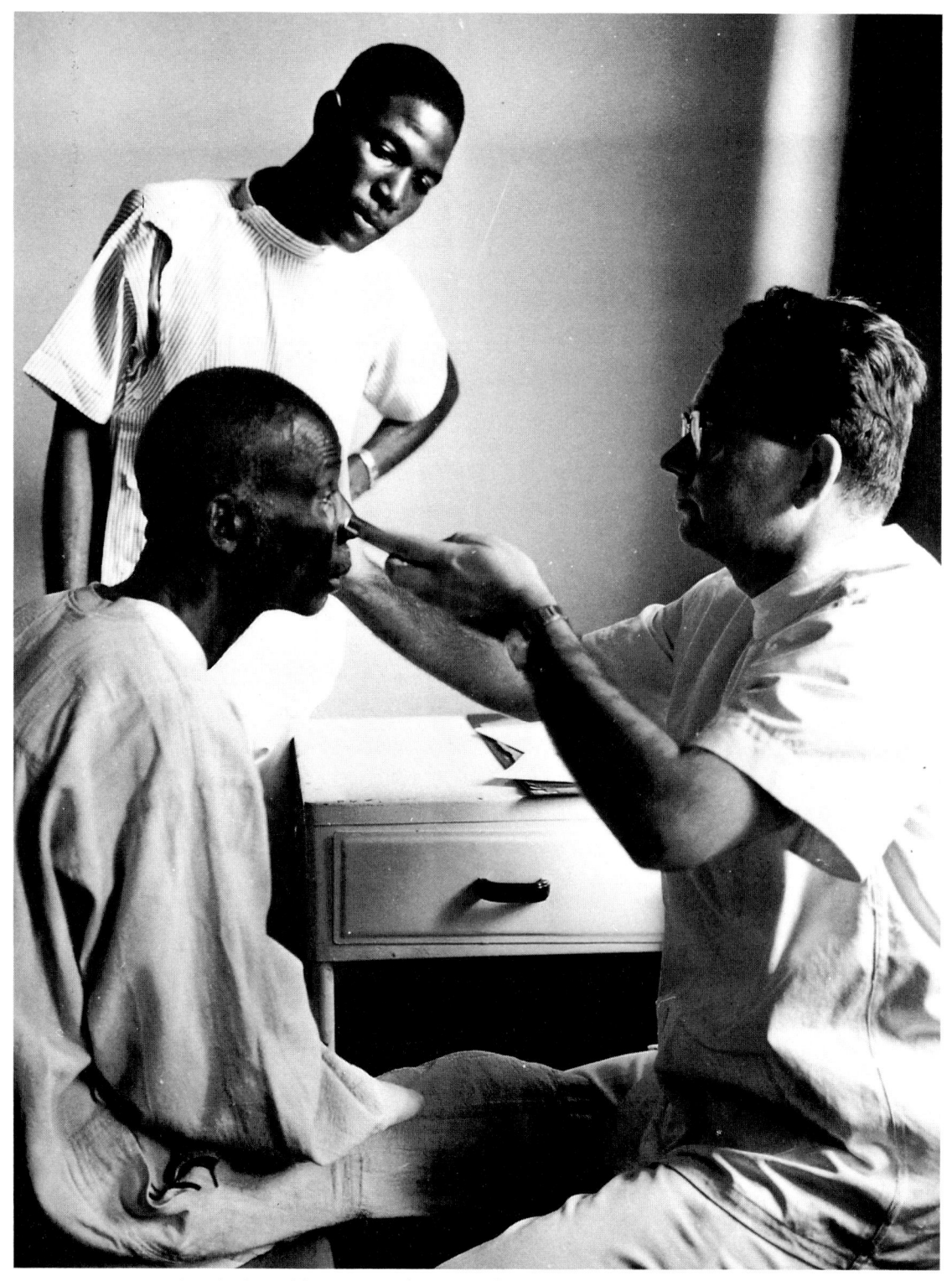

67 Aid to the Third World: at an eye clinic in Malawi, an Israeli doctor examines a patient while a local student looks on.

employed. Begun on a very small scale in Burma and Ghana in the 1960s, Israeli technical aid spread across three continents; by the end of 1971, some 5,000 Israeli experts had been sent on such missions by the Government; some 15,000 trainees had come to Israel from much of the Third World for all manner of instruction. The pace was to slacken; the programmes to be decimated in 1973, following the Yom Kippur War. But, in the meantime, who could better help institutions struggling to enter the twentieth century on their own – after generations of foreign rule – that these zealous young Israelis, free of colonial taint, wanting only friendship and perhaps admiration openly arrived at and openly declared, anxious to teach and capable of learning?

The traffic was two-way; Israelis and their families left for the Ivory Coast, Tanganyika, Gabon and Kenya; Africans and Asians arrived for training at Israeli hospitals, universities, agricultural colleges and centres. Hebrew often became, incongruously, the one language that a would-be pharmacist from French-speaking Africa could possibly share with an English-speaking paratrooper from the Congo. Furthermore, Israelis were not pampered; they complained less than most other non-natives about difficult living conditions, unfamiliar food, the problems encountered by their children. They quickly picked up local songs, dances and customs, and could not wait to demonstrate their own. They built hotels, schools, and eye clinics; explained what a kibbutz was and how it operated, and about Israel's Nahal which combined military service with work on the land. The experiment, launched rather gingerly, succeeded beyond anyone's wildest dreams. 'It was, I think, the most important contribution I made as Israel's Foreign Minister,' Golda Meir was to sum up. 'I am prouder ... of the assistance we gave the people of Africa than I am of any other single project we have ever undertaken.' Over and above its obvious virtues for all concerned, the Technical Aid Programme widened horizons for the Israelis who took part in it, lessened the frustration of being ringed by perpetually hostile neighbours and, at least temporarily, substituted an ocean of friends for a sea of enemies.

In 1963, David Ben-Gurion resigned finally as Israel's Prime Minister. He had held that position, serving also as Minister of Defence, for most of the time that had lapsed since he proclaimed Israel a sovereign state in 1948. His stocky body, topped by flyaway white hair, his bright eyes roofed by bushy eyebrows, his brisk walk and characteristically abrupt way of talking, rendered him instantly recognizable, the delight of cartoonists. Tough, sure of himself, controlling, interested in everything from biblical exegesis to building better barracks, he was born in Poland in 1886, at seventeen already the founder of a Zionist group and two years later active in Jewish self-defence organized in the wake of the anti-Jewish pogroms in 1903. In 1906, he left for Palestine where he helped lay the foundations of the labour movement of which he became the virtually unchallenged leader and boss, both within the Labour Party itself and in the Histadrut. However, it is as Premier that he played a possibly indispensable role; if not the father of the Jewish state, then certainly during those first determining fifteen years, B.G. (as he was called except by familiars who spoke of him as The Old Man) was its canny, infuriating and inspiring Chief Executive Officer – both metaphorically and literally. His immediate influence on the burgeoning of the state was immense, although the passage of time and the press of events have perhaps eroded its impact.

An ardent believer in the future of the Negev, in cultivating one's own garden rather than just adding to its size, and in setting a personal example, he realized all three goals in 1963 by joining a tiny desert kibbutz, Sde Boker, in which he spent the rest of his life. For several years, he worked as a kibbutz shepherd, elderly but diligent, reading and writing late into the night and continuing to express himself forcefully, often critically, on domestic and foreign affairs. He is buried at Sde Boker, now a place of pilgrimage for his still-mourning followers and VIP visitors to the country. The last years of his political life were coloured by the Lavon Affair and the question of who was to blame for a tragic failure of Israeli intelligence in Egypt. The actual security blunder took place in 1954 when, briefly, Moshe Sharett was Prime Minister, Pinhas Lavon Defence Minister and Ben-Gurion down in Sde Boker on a leave-of-absence. Lavon, denying any knowledge of the operation, resigned; Sharett went back to being Israel's Foreign Minister; and B.G. was hastily summoned first to the Defence Ministry, then, following the elections of 1955, he reassumed also the Prime Ministership. Five years later, the Affair became a major *cause célèbre*; the ensuing scandals within the Labour Party resulting in the formation of break-away splinter groups to the accompaniment of charges and counter-charges, again having to do with 'Who gave the order?'. Lavon demanded that Ben-Gurion publicly clear his (Lavon's) name; B.G. absolutely refused. A commission of seven cabinet ministers then exonerated Lavon, but B.G. wouldn't accept their decision. He recommended Levi Eshkol as his successor, resigned and returned to Sde Boker.

In 1964, the Lavon Affair made headlines again. At this point, B.G. was a Knesset member heading a small party which included Moshe Dayan and

68 In 'retirement', David Ben-Gurion tends docile new charges at Kibbutz Sde Boker, founded in 1952 as a frontier outpost.

69 One aftermath of the Lavon Affair: former Israeli agent Wolfgang Lotz makes an appearance at the 1971 wedding of another Israeli agent, Marcelle Ninio, also released from an Egyptian jail after the Six Day War. The bride was given away by Prime Minister Golda Meir (left).

Shimon Peres; insisting that a judicial inquiry be held and the Lavon Affair reinvestigated, he lashed out not only at Eshkol but at anyone who disagreed with him regarding the alleged cover-up. Unable to get his way, he went back to the desert, from there persisting in his fight on behalf of what he termed truth, justice and the due processes of law. During the years of his leadership, he called also for other things: for peace, which he believed depended more on increasing the number of Jews in Israel than it did on having more territory; for Israel to become 'a light unto the nations', unique in its ethical values, compassion and intellectual vitality; and for Israelis to act in their own best interests rather than be governed by what the 'gentile' world thinks. Much of this vision has yet to be realized, but it well may be that, in centuries to come, historians surveying the *raison d'être* and first steps of the Jewish state will mention only Theodor Herzl and David Ben-Gurion.

Apart from the history-altering decision taken by the Yishuv in 1948, no subsequent events in the short annals of the State of Israel had so reverberating or abiding an effect as did the Six Day War between Israel and Egypt, Jordan, Syria and Iraq, which lasted from 5 June to 10 June 1967. It resulted in the occupation by Israel of the entire Sinai Peninsula, the so-called West Bank and the Golan Heights, thereby changing (for the foreseeable future) the order of things as they had been in the Middle East for nearly twenty years.

For the ruler of Egypt, Gamal Abdel Nasser, the early spring of 1967 was an uneasy time; for years, his troops had been involved in a pointless war in Yemen; his relationship with King Hussein of Jordan had deteriorated into name-calling ('Hashemite harlot' being one genealogical epithet hurled from Cairo to Amman); he was not getting along well with Saudi Arabia and, worst of all, was making no headway in his frequently enunciated aim of obliterating Israel, defined by him as the arch-enemy of all Arabs. He was forty-nine and a man of action; he had led the military revolution which, fifteen years earlier, had destroyed Egypt's ruling class, ended the seventy years of British rule in Egypt, won control of the Suez Canal, inaugurated the Aswan Dam and begun to modernize Egypt. Inaction was anathema to him — and yet here he was, stalemated in so many areas. The stalemate, however, was soon to be broken.

The Russians, ever on the alert for trouble in the Middle East and anxious to help out the Syrians, their newest friends in the vicinity, came along with an entirely fabricated story: Israeli brigades, they reported, were massing ominously on the Syrian frontier. Nothing, including a visit to the northern border pressed on the Soviet Ambassador to Israel by Prime Minister Eshkol himself, did any good; the Syrians, well-coached, maintained that a major offensive against them was indeed being prepared. By the beginning of May, the Arab world was in the grip of mass hysteria; some 100,000 troops (and over 1,000 tanks) were waiting in Sinai along the Israeli border, with Radio Cairo repeatedly and shrilly assuring everyone of Egyptian readiness for 'the total war that will spell the end of Israel'. All that stood between the frenzied Arabs and the doomed Israelis, so Nasser seems to have thought, was the presence of the United Nations Emergency Force at Sharm el-Sheikh and the Gaza Strip; remove that and victory was his; so he asked the UN to remove it, a request with which the Secretary-General of that organization at once, and inexplicably, complied.

The next step was to close the Straits of Tiran to Israeli shipping and shipping bound to and from Israel. That done, caught up in the orgy of hatred, some long-fantasized triumph over Israel now within his reach, deftly erasing the memory of Nasser's abuse and casting all caution to the winds, King Hussein joined the fray – though the recipient of constant communications from Israel promising that no harm would come to Jordan if he just kept out of the way. He put his forces under Egyptian command; within days, the Jordanians were joined by soldiers from Iraq, Kuwait and Algeria, bringing the Arab force up to 250,000, doubling the number of tanks.

In Israel it was thought inconceivable – almost inconceivable, that is – that the Western powers would remain aloof from what was clearly the tightening of a noose around the Jewish state. But little comfort could be found in the flurry of formal statements or in the answers that Foreign Minister Abba Eban was getting as he visited Paris, London and Washington, asking whether these nations had any intention of honouring the guarantees they had given to Israel in 1956. The replies were vaguely worded at best, but the message was unmistakable: Israel would have to go it alone, defend her right to exist, pit resources against a huge war machine powered by maddened mobs from throughout the Arab world, and not count on any old promises. What had to be understood and faced was that there would be war – and that, once again, there would be no alternative but to win it.

Daily life was adjusted accordingly: all men and transport, capable of serving, were mobilized; the over-age and the young were set vital tasks, tending crops, helping out in hospitals and with mail deliveries, filling sandbags with which to line doorways and digging ditches in gardens; long-neglected basements were turned out and into makeshift air-raid shelters;

each household prepared blackouts at night and kept an emergency kit ready – for what? Who knew? Other accommodations were made: in response to public pressure, General Moshe Dayan was appointed Israel's Minister of Defence on 3 June 1967. Cocky, fearless and talented, a soldier who understood the nature of the enemy, of the terrain and of war, and who epitomized authority, surefootedness and freedom from convention, he seemed the best man around in this time of troubles, most Israelis seeing in him a symbol of the Land itself, a modern David who could be relied on to wield a wicked slingshot against the Goliath of 1967. Never mind that Prime Minister Eshkol, in his capacity as Minister of Defence (and other earlier capacities), had quietly made possible the efficiency and modernity of Israel's army or that he too was endowed with sound judgment and impressive experience, and was grievously hurt by the demand for Dayan. Dayan, however, held no monopoly on the nation's confidence; it was reposited also with the Chief of Staff, General Yitzhak Rabin, and, above all, with the citizen army itself. It was perhaps this solidarity, and the political unity expressed by a wall-to-wall national coalition, that won for Israel, during those tense days of waiting for something to happen, the unqualified and emotional support of world Jewry, drawing thousands of volunteers, almost none of whom were accepted, to its consulates and embassies.

Early in the morning of 5 June, the situation changed. Moving in a sudden massive pre-emptive attack, within three hours the Israel Air Force had destroyed the air forces (more than 400 planes on the ground) and the airfields of Egypt, Syria and Jordan, and, in combat, done away with another sixty Arab planes. The skies were now Israel's; the noose was cut. The war was not over but Israelis, barely believing the news, took deep breaths, and most, each in his or her own way, thanked God for the deliverance.

The mailed fist was free to close, to hammer at the Arab land forces; by the end of Day One, Israeli armour was far into Sinai, *en route* to the Canal, and at the outskirts of Gaza. That same day, a last reminder went off to Jordan: Israel had no designs on the Hashemite kingdom; let there just be quiet on the Israel–Jordan border. But Hussein moved, for him, fatally: the attack by the Jordanian Arab Legion on Jerusalem and Jewish border settlements cost him the Old City of Jerusalem, in Jordanian hands since 1948, and lost him the area known in Israel today as Judea and Samaria (or the West Bank), seventy miles long and thirty miles wide. Within less than a week, the Israeli flag was raised at the Suez Canal; the Straits of Tiran were open; the Egyptian troops in demoralized flight; the Golan Heights taken after bloody battles; and the Israel Defence Forces established on the road to Damascus. There were bills to be paid, of course: independence and survival, however bravely and dramatically won, were not gratis; Israel's losses were nearly 800 killed and close to 3,000 wounded (as opposed to some 15,000 Arab casualties), and a handful of prisoners later released in return for nearly 6,000 Arab prisoners of war.

Eighty hours of combat had placed under Israel's control 47,000 square miles, an area six times larger than Israel itself. What would happen now? No one knew, so in the interim, Israelis rejoiced at the liberation of the Old City, wept at the Wailing Wall, went sightseeing on an unprecedented scale, travelling from Mount Hermon to Sharm el-Sheikh, through Nablus, Hebron and Jericho, in and out of Sinai, and back again and again to the Old City of Jerusalem. Nor were the excursions all one-way: Arabs from the territories visited Tel Aviv in droves; those who felt like it went all over Israel free of restriction. But most non-Israeli Arabs, knowing who had won and who had lost, kept to themselves; many closed businesses, shuttered shops, said goodbye to friends and left for abroad to start life again elsewhere, while in Israel, along with the joy and the wonder, there were those who began to ponder the consequences of conquest, to discuss their reactions to war and to the thousands of Arabs for whose welfare, within one week, they had become – to one degree or another – responsible.

About one thing, all Israelis (except the Communists) agreed: this time nothing would be given back for free; there would be no premature return of an inch of land; the price of the territories would be peace, an end for ever to armed conflict. It did not come about. In September 1967, at the Arab Summit meeting held in Khartoum, the collective response was negative: 'No recognition of Israel. No negotiations with Israel. No peace.' Nothing had changed, after all, even after three wars and twenty years. Not only this, but a fourth war was already being planned.

The Egyptian War of Attrition against Israel, intended to wear down the renewed Israeli determination, was waged from the spring of 1969 to the summer of 1970 along the Suez Canal ceasefire line. It took the form of merciless shelling, and of Jordanian army and Palestinian terrorist operations in the administered areas and, to some extent, within Israel proper. Everywhere it failed, but it was not painless.

True, not one Israeli stronghold along the Canal was dislodged and,

70 Above: Young Jews from Canada and the US rushed to volunteer for work in Israeli settlements and hospitals as soon as the Six Day War broke out. It ended too quickly for most of them to serve.

71 Opposite top: Israeli troops manning IDF outposts controlling the Suez Canal swing-bridge at Al Firdan, June 1967.

72 Opposite below: Toppling the wall that divided Jerusalem.

73 Overleaf: Draped in a prayer shawl, an Orthodox soldier dutifully pauses in the desert for prayer, June 1967.

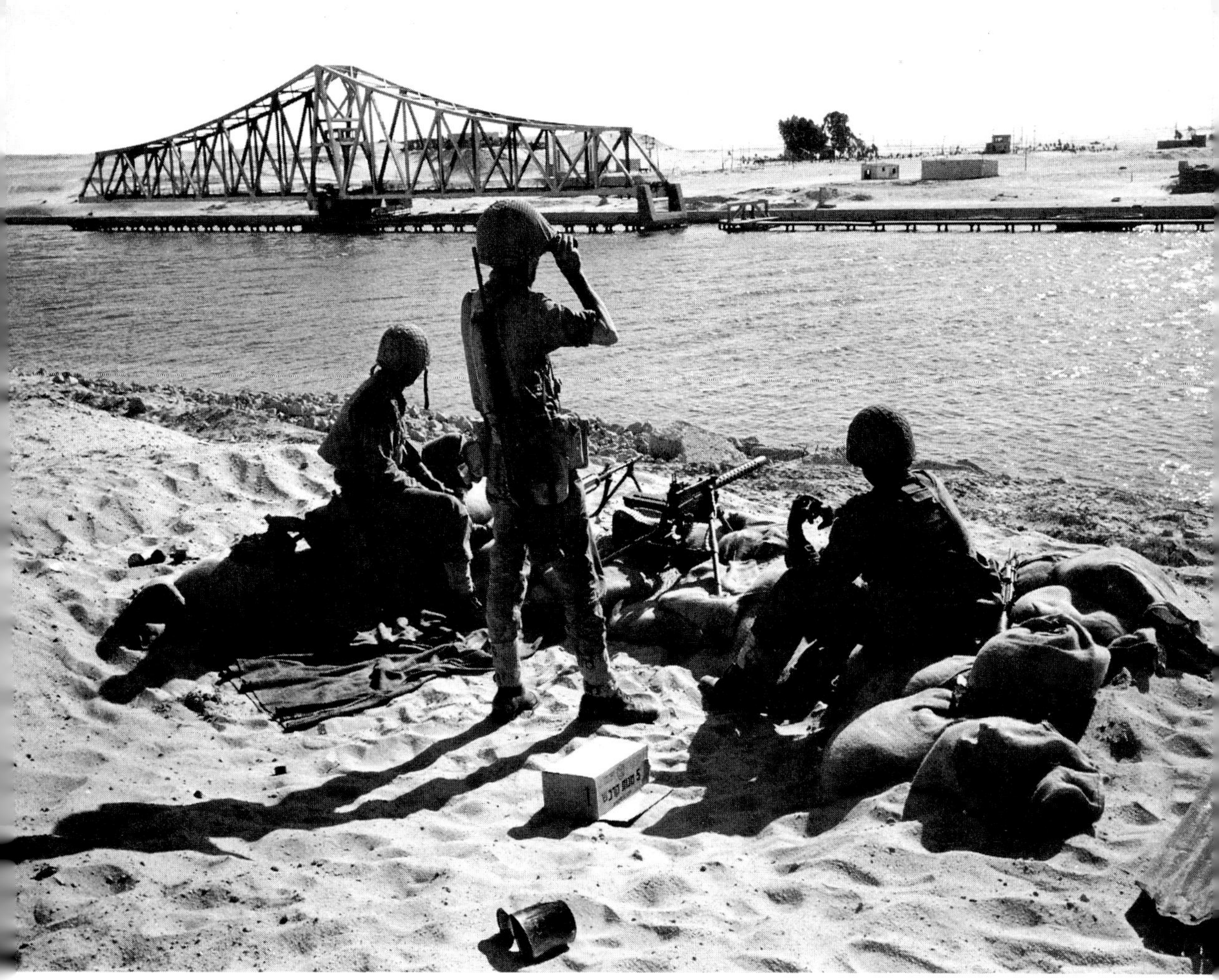

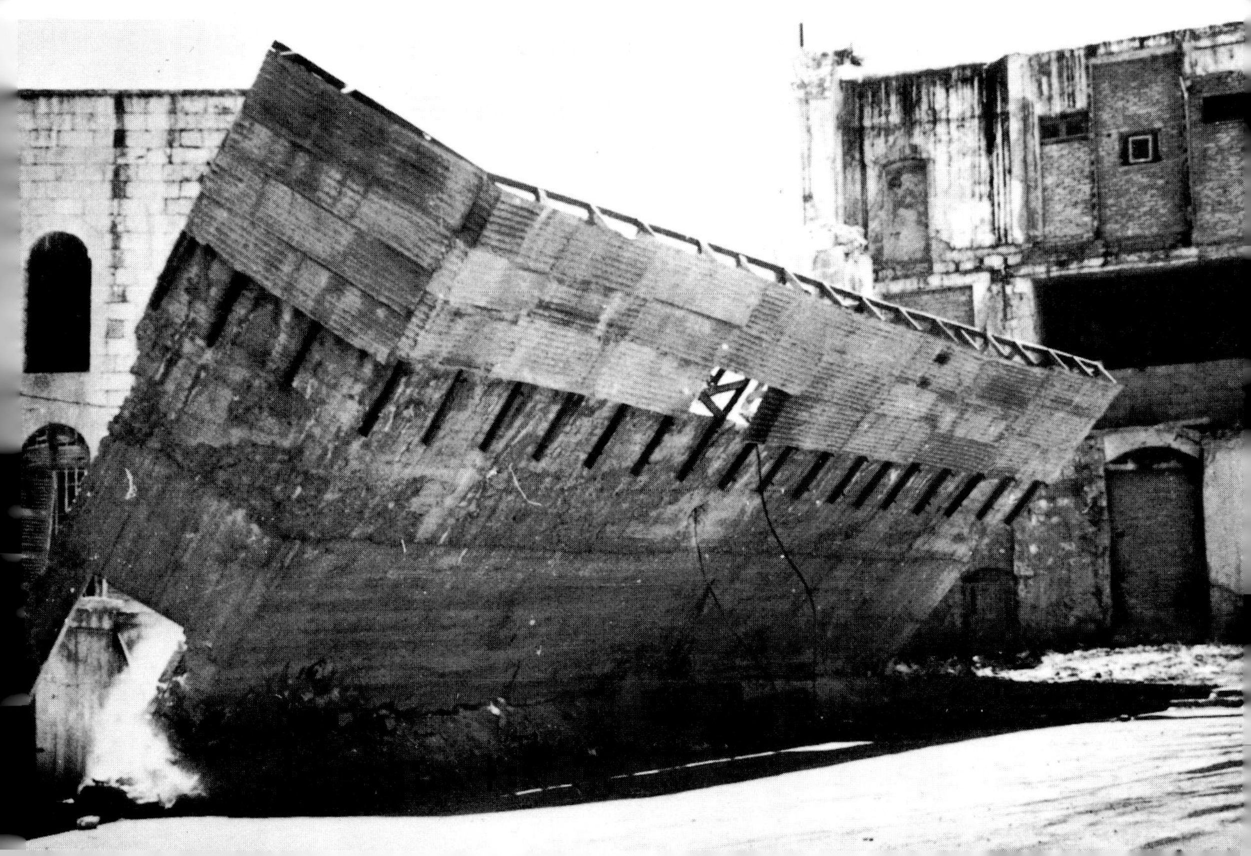

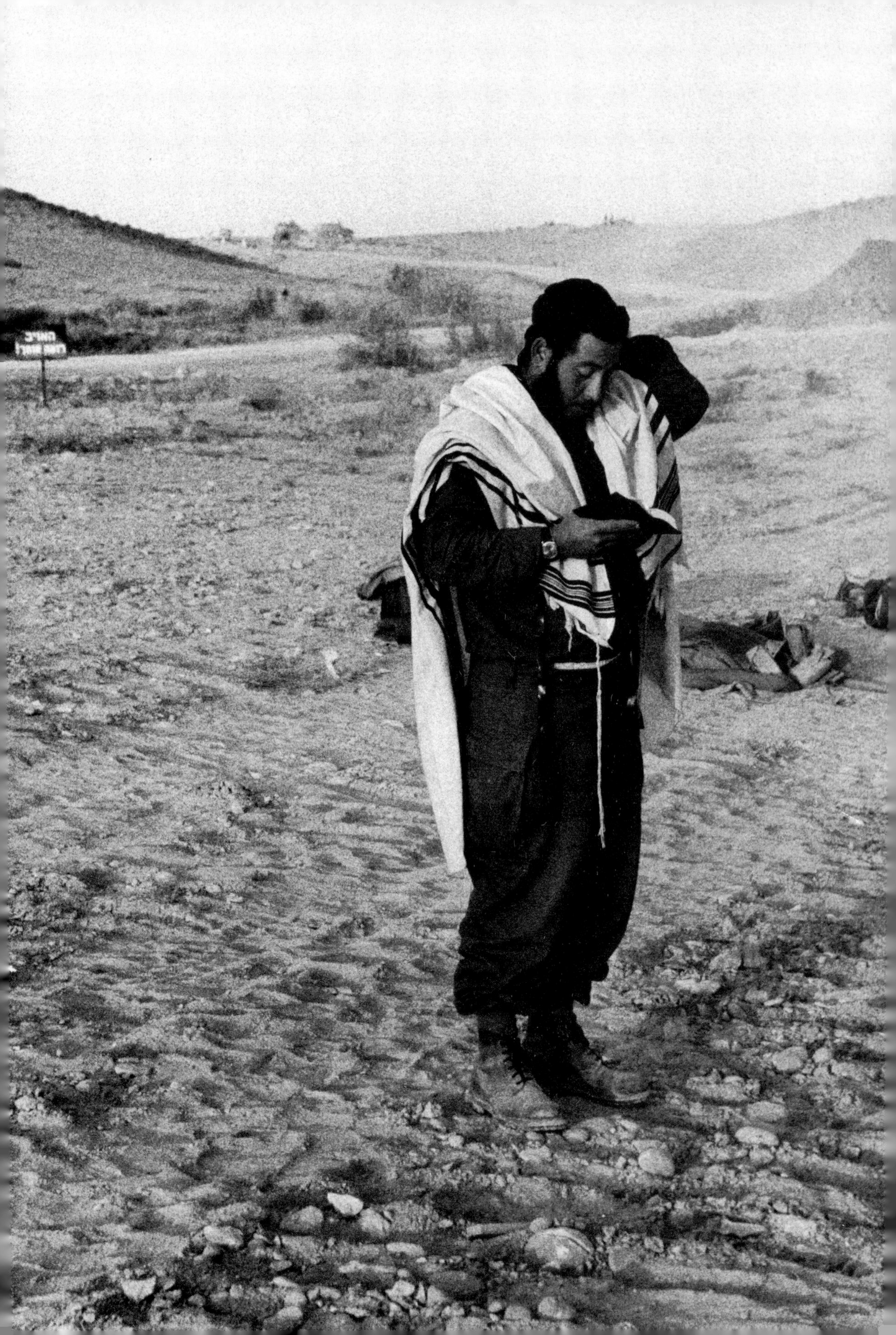

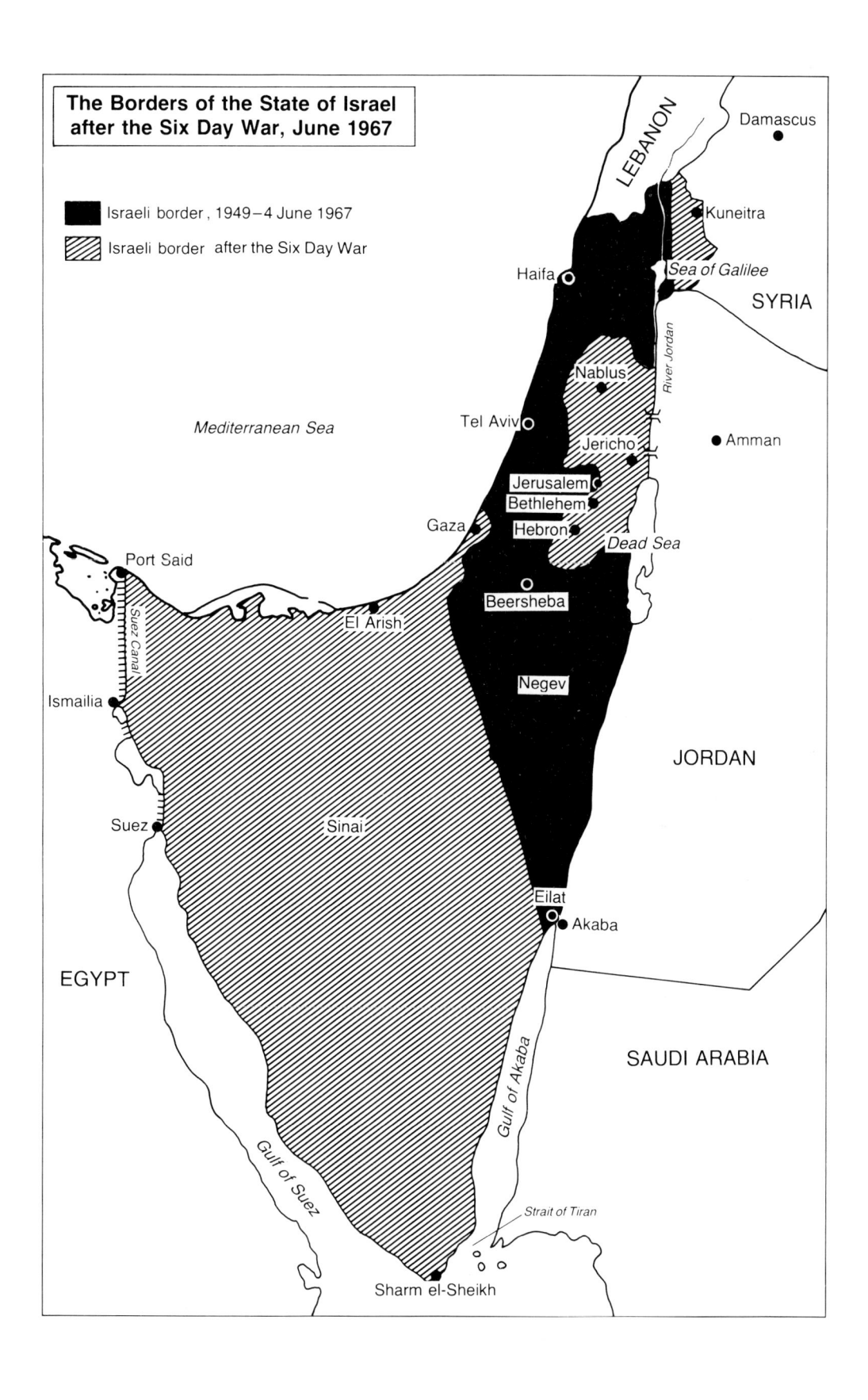

The Borders of the State of Israel after the Six Day War, June 1967

true, the Israel Air Force turned itself into a fearsome flying artillery, pounding Egyptian positions, while Israeli commando raids penetrated the Nile Valley and military installations in Cairo. But having and keeping the upper hand did not mean that the long-term problem was any nearer solution, and there were Israeli casualties, always a source of national anguish.

The Bar-Lev Line, a chain of Israeli fortifications, was laboriously strung along the length of the Canal, but compared with the gifts the Egyptians were getting from their Soviet sponsors — ground-to-air missiles and the personnel to work them — the situation did not appear promising. Finally, under United States and United Nations auspices, various provisional ceasefire agreements were concluded, broken and renewed. In 1971, Egypt's new President Anwar Sadat officially declared that he would no longer extend the last ceasefire, but the fighting did stop; in 1972, Sadat threw most of the Russian military personnel out of Egypt and the prospects of unending war in the Middle East dimmed, though terror was much in dreadful evidence. It began to look as though Sadat might play a decisive role, one way or the other.

CHAPTER 8

The Noose Tightens: Terrorism, War and Victory

The years between the Six Day War and the Yom Kippur War of 1973 gave no early warning of the enormous changes which would take place in the self-image, leadership and priorities of Israeli society. It was natural, of course, in a population so given to ideological debate and dissent, that there be prophets of doom, so-called 'doves' who wrote, spoke and marched on behalf of less rigid Israeli approaches to the attainment of peace. Warning that holding on to the 'conquered' territories would, in the long run and inevitably, distort the ideals of the state, and add yet another obstacle to any prospect of Israel's acceptance by the Arabs, they were loud in their condemnation of arrangements whereby some 55,000 Arabs from the West Bank and Gaza worked in Israel (mostly in construction and agriculture) as 'hewers of wood and drawers of water', doing the manual work that the Founding Fathers of Zionism had so ardently believed should be undertaken in the Land by Jews.

Fundamentally opposed to this Peace Now movement and its several variations was the religious bloc, whose members, albeit in differing degrees, believed that the borders of the Land of Israel were defined for ever in the Bible; that nothing promised therein – and returned to after so long – could possibly be lost once more to the Chosen People.

Between those poles were the less militant 'hawks' and the more hard-headed 'doves', i.e. the majority of Israelis, who saw the territories as representing what might be Israel's last chance to force the Arab states to negotiate peace with secure and defensible borders – and thus as acquisitions certainly to be held on to for the time being.

Since the Arab states were committed to bringing about Israel's withdrawal by all means *other* than negotiation, in reality the various ornithological distinctions within Israel itself made little difference but, as the months passed, polarization of opinion became increasingly acute, the ceaseless argument ever more impassioned.

A new brand of Arab terrorism emerged during this period; supported by the Soviet Union and a bevy of the more affluent Arab states (Libya notable among them), it was derived partly from the *fedayeen* of the 1950s, partly from the 1964 founding, in Egypt, of the Palestine Liberation Organization (PLO). Glorying in its intimate ties, financial and spiritual, with such organizations as the Irish Republican Army (IRA), Italy's Red Brigades, the Basque ETA and the Japanese Red Army, the PLO claimed its victims not only in Israel or on the borders but wherever, and however, it chose, in this way ensuring constant media exposure – provided that the killing, kidnapping and hijacking were carried out in sufficiently spectacular ways. Despite the scope and wantonness of the terror, and the sinister international connections of the terrorists, the West was remarkably slow to take action against the PLO or other smaller Arab terrorist groups linked to it, though between 1965 and 1982, 326 people were killed and 768 wounded outside Israel, forty non-Israeli civilian planes commandeered or attacked, and passengers machine-gunned, at random, in five major airports. For Israel, one of the most horrifying of these murders was the PLO slaughter of eleven Israeli athletes at the 1972 Olympics in Munich; the Hitler-associated locale, the mockery made of the much-vaunted Olympics spirit of fair play, the fact that the murders were televised 'live', and the insistence of the Olympics management that the games continue as though nothing untoward had happened, all served to underscore the outrage and heighten the sense of peril that now routinely accompanied Israelis travelling or serving abroad.

Stress, and no small measure of hazard, also characterized the state's finances: taxation, direct and indirect, was among the highest anywhere in the world; inflation, not yet galloping, was already alarming; the trade deficit still widening; and the Israeli pound so rapidly declining that, in 1975, there would be a whopping devaluation of 43 per cent, doubling and trebling the cost of everything. None the less, as the decade opened, the prevailing mood was one of confidence. Even in Israel, life is not lived entirely at fever-pitch; most people, possibly with more cause than elsewhere, are expert in the counting of blessings, assets and silver linings – and despite the tensions and instabilities, several were to be found.

Prime Minister Golda Meir was very popular: her plain speaking, intelligence,

74 An IDF officer asks for the co-operation of Arab villagers, 1968. The Six Day War brought under Israeli surveillance and administration some one million Arabs, including about 600,000 inhabitants of Judea and Samaria.

75 Hundreds of thousands of Arabs, many from states at war with Israel, have crossed the Jordan River bridges or landed at Ben-Gurion airport since 1967 to visit families in Israel and the administered territories.

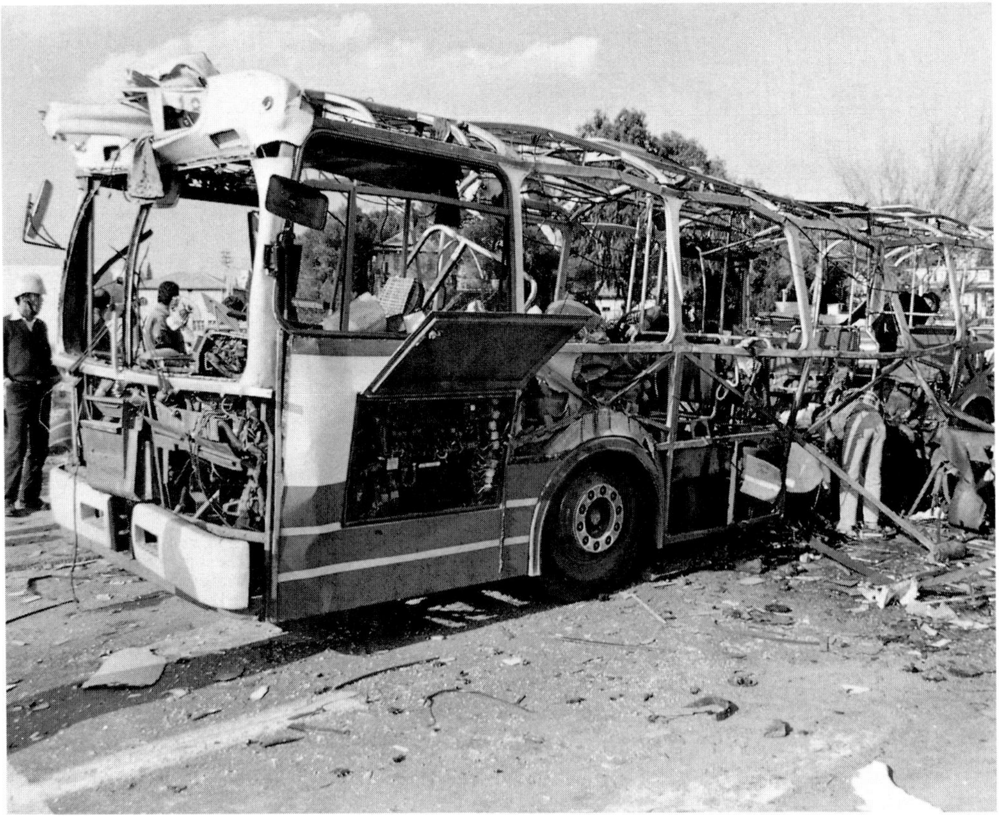

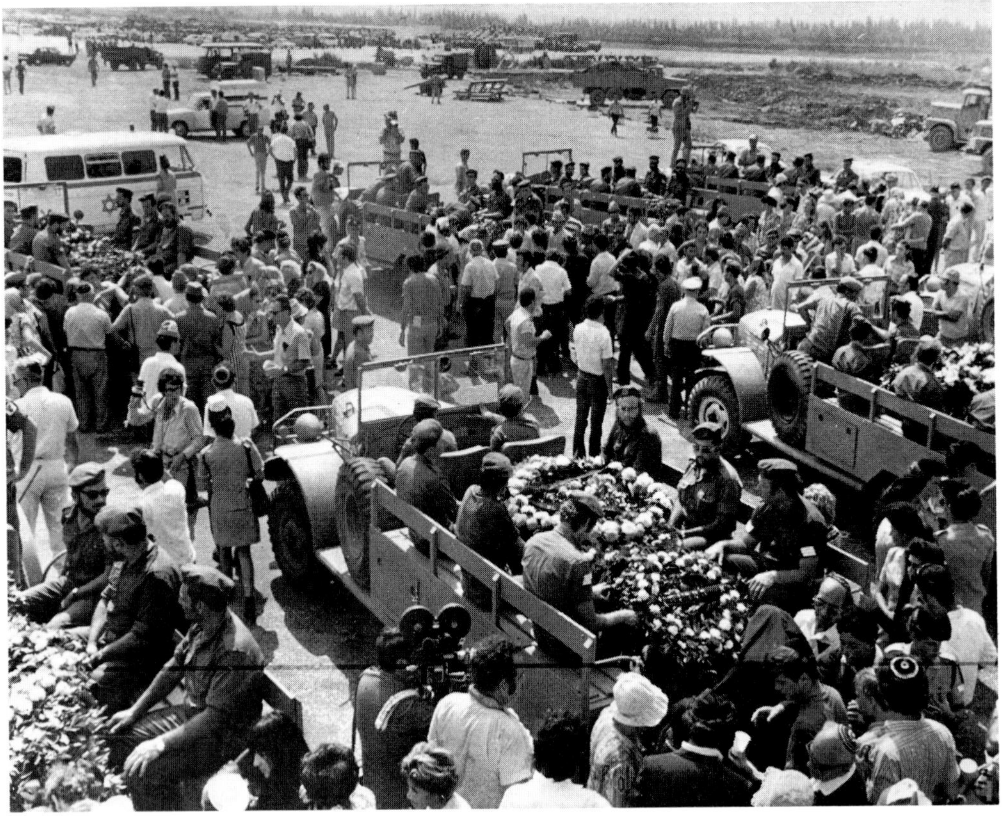

78 A group of Soviet Jews arrive in Israel from Moscow, one of them tenderly clasping the Scrolls of the Law, 1972.

76 Opposite top: What a PLO terrorist attack on a Jerusalem bus looks like, shortly afterwards.

77 Opposite below: The coffins of the ten Israelis killed in the Munich Olympics massacre arrive at Ben-Gurion airport, July 1972.

common sense and humour endeared her to the average citizen as did her stand (labelled 'intransigence' by critics from within and without) opposing the return of territory except as against the promise of peace. 'I believe', she wrote before she died in 1978, 'that we will have peace with our neighbours, but I am quite sure that no one will make peace with a weak Israel.' She became Prime Minister when Levi Eshkol died in 1969: 'I could certainly understand the reservations of people who thought that a seventy-year-old grandmother was hardly ... perfect ... to head a twenty-year-old state,' she once commented. But, in fact, she had been a Labour Party and Histadrut stalwart for many years, later Israel's Labour Minister, and afterwards Foreign Minister, and she was a seasoned and skilful politician, whose American accent (Russian-born, she was raised in Milwaukee), uncompromising hair-do and capacious handbags were universally recognized-and-relished trademarks.

In 1973, Israel acquired a new, eminently suitable President, Professor Ephraim Katzir, a renowned biophysicist whose scientist brother had been shot to death the year before during a terrorist attack at Lod airport (in which twenty-one Christian pilgrims also died). For many Israelis, it was a source of satisfaction, as the state celebrated its twenty-fifth anniversary, that the fourth President, like his three predecessors, was a man of high intellectual achievement who, though he had served, among other posts, as Chief Scientist of the Defence Ministry, embodied not ongoing involvement with military matters, but rather the search for knowledge that better befitted the People of the Book.

Another item at the top of the national progress report concerned immigration. Following the Six Day War, a wave of newcomers had arrived, chiefly from the Americas and Western Europe but also from the Soviet Union. Between June 1967 and June 1975, a total of 103,000 Soviet Jews came to Israel, including hundreds of professionals who had to find jobs (frequently outside their specialities), make the adjustment to a wholly different society and land, and face some initial antagonism from more veteran immigrants, mainly those who came in the 1950s from North Africa and resented the greater efficiency and comfort with which the Russians were welcomed. Some Russian Jews reached Israel, spent an obligatory few months there and then took off as soon as they could for the West, but thousands upon thousands stayed, the difficulties attendant upon their integration dwarfed by the burning desire to live freely as Jews which had enabled them to survive years of official Soviet chastisement, deprived of employment, all-too-often exiled to Siberian penal labour camps. Periodic carping aside, all

Israel rejoiced that these Jews — ruthlessly cut off from the mainstream of Jewish life, their Zionism nurtured in isolation, their Judaism prohibited and punished — were at last among the Ingathered.

There were also less but still meaningful successes: Israel signed a preferential trade agreement with the European Common Market; the state was now party to over 600 bilateral agreements (friendship, culture, technical assistance, etc.) with close to 100 countries and nine major international organizations; a batch of science-based industries had been born, developed and was doing very well; Israeli fine instruments, bathing-suits, melons and roses were in demand throughout Europe and major department stores abroad were featuring 'Israel Weeks'. Tourism had brought some 800,000 visitors to Israel in 1972 and was expected to bring that figure to one million within a year or so. Not least, Israelis applauded the reduction of compulsory military service for men from thirty-six to thirty-three months, and, reflecting Israel's other persona, the award to writer S. Y. Agnon of the Nobel Prize for Literature. Under the circumstances, so far, so good was the general feeling — if only terrorism would come to an end and the Arabs agree to talk.

In September 1973, Israeli Intelligence noted more-than-routine activity on the Egyptian and Syrian fronts. Although the Arab war machine was not regarded as much of a menace since its total disablement in the Six Day War, Israel's military presence in the north and south was intensified to be on the safe side, the reinforcement of enemy troops explained as the result of Syrian nervousness. On 4 October, more disturbing information was received, having to do with the hasty preparations being made for the sudden return home of the families of Soviet advisers in Syria — for no known reason. Golda Meir was uneasy about this news but the Minister of Defence, the Chief of Staff and the head of Military Intelligence reassured her: there was no cause, they said, for special worry. None the less, a cabinet meeting was called for midday, Friday 5 October. This was not an ordinary Friday; it was the eve of Yom Kippur, the Day of Atonement, the holiest, most solemn day of the Jewish calendar, twenty-four hours which almost all Jews, wherever they are, mark in one way or another, traditionally by prayer and fasting, or by not going to work and not eating in public.

As for Israel, it closes down on Yom Kippur. Today, news is broadcast; in 1973, not even that; there was no radio, no transportation, and only skeleton staffs where absolutely essential. At the Friday meeting, again 'no one seemed very alarmed', to quote Golda Meir, though it *was* decided that,

79 Throughout the 1970s, crates of choice Israeli citrus journeyed to hundreds of export markets abroad. In the 1980s several new Israeli-developed tropical fruits successfully joined Israel's noted melons, strawberries and avocados.

if indeed necessary, the Prime Minister and the Defence Minister could order a full-scale call-up. At 4 a.m. on Saturday 6 October, intelligence reported that the Egyptians and the Syrians would launch a co-ordinated attack on Israel at six o'clock that afternoon. By 10 a.m., mobilization of Israel's armed forces commenced. The Arab attack, however, was launched not at 6 p.m. but four hours earlier, at 2 p.m.! Israel was taken by surprise.

The mistakes and misreadings were grave, only to be understood in the light of Israel's overall underestimation of the Arab need, and desire, for revenge; the equivalent overestimation of Israeli infallibility; and the general complacency bolstered by what bordered on contempt for Arab military performance. The price paid for these was exorbitant: summoned from homes and synagogues to answer the call to arms, 2,522 Israelis never returned; and in the first two or three days of the war, only the thinnest line of brave men stood between the state and disaster. Speaking to a public that did not yet know what was happening – only that, most ominously, there had been a call-up on Yom Kippur – Golda Meir addressed the citizens of Israel in a telecast that gave no clue, save for the exceptional severity of her expression, to the real dimensions of the calamity. 'We do not doubt,' she said, 'that we shall prevail.' Moshe Dayan also spoke: 'it will end in a few days with victory'. Outside, the roads were jammed with traffic: buses, trucks and private cars were taking soldiers, many with prayer shawls still draped over their shoulders, to join their units.

The war was fought on two fronts, simultaneously. On the Golan Heights, formation after formation of Syrian aircraft swooped over Israeli positions as hundreds of Syrian tanks, four abreast, rolled into devastating action. It took five days of relentless fighting for the tide to turn; on the night of 6 October, the Syrians were on routes leading to the Sea of Galilee; by 10 October, battered, exhausted, suffering heavy losses, the Israelis were already pushing eastwards over the Syrians' own lines, on the road to Damascus. Despite counter-attacks by Syrian, Iraqi and Jordanian forces, despite the initial capture of Mount Hermon and the failure of a number of Israeli assaults, by 22 October Mount Hermon was again in Israeli hands, the Syrian air force critically hurt, the Syrian Soviet-donated SAM-6 and SAM-7 missile systems (not previously encountered by the Israelis) largely destroyed and the Syrian command ready to accept the ceasefire requested by the UN Security Council. Over-eager participation in Y-Day (an Arab code-name for 6 October) cost Syria some 1,100 tanks (many the latest USSR model), 3,500 dead and hundreds of prisoners of war.

The massive Egyptian attack on the sixteen strongholds of Israel's Bar-Lev Line of fortifications strung out along the Suez Canal was – on that Yom Kippur day – met by some five hundred or so reservists who were outnumbered two hundred to one, each stronghold fighting its own last-ditch battle. Not only had the Line proved the opposite of impregnable but a secret device, installed to heighten its supposed impregnability, had failed to work. At 2 p.m. on 6 October, some 70,000 Egyptian troops (a few days earlier thought by the Israelis to be part of an extensive Egyptian military exercise) crossed the Canal, taking up positions on the eastern bank which were intended for Israeli armour. By nightfall, the Egyptians had ferried five divisions of infantry and armour across the water and set up three major bridgeheads, all under the cover of mobile anti-aircraft and anti-tank missile systems which wreaked havoc on Israeli planes and took scores of Israeli lives as the IDF struggled to relieve units trapped in the Bar-Lev Line. Some of the Line's defenders managed, against dreadful odds, to hold out for several days, but most of the fortifications were taken by the Egyptians – or abandoned. The war did not look in the least as though it would end in a few days.

On the fifth day, the Syrians having been pushed back across the 1967 ceasefire line, the war cabinet considered urgent matters of crossing the Canal, the possible duration of the war and the spectre of running out of planes, tanks and ammunitions. US President Richard Nixon promised his assistance, though the US Defense Department was, at first, not particularly enthusiastic about the idea of an airlift. The clock ticked away while gigantic quantities of Soviet military aircraft arrived daily in Egypt, Syria and Iraq; on the ninth day of the war, the first flight of the great US c-5 Galaxies finally landed at Lydda. 'I cried for the first time since the war began, though not the last,' wrote Golda Meir. It was also the day on which the first casualty lists were published in Israel.

The air lift not only boosted morale but it clarified the US stand and, with the Phantom and Skyhawk planes that also followed, it made possible the mounting of lethal Israeli counter-attacks. On the night of 15 October, Israel's forces crossed the Canal and established themselves, against fierce Egyptian resistance, on that waterway's west bank, in Egypt proper, in some of a cruel war's cruellest engagements. By 22 October, Israeli units were in the Egyptian town of Ismailia and on the Cairo–Suez road, had encircled the 20,000 soldiers of Egypt's Third Army, and moved into the town of Suez – under Egyptian fire and with many losses. On 24 October, the Egyptians

80 The Yom Kippur War of 1973: Israeli tanks on pontoon bridges roll across the Suez Canal.

81 The Yom Kippur battles were bitter, bloody and costly but ended, from the military point of view, in victory for the IDF.

had two bridgeheads on the eastern bank of the Canal – to a depth of roughly ten kilometres; the Israelis occupied about 1,600 square kilometres inside Egypt, a stretch of land they took to calling 'Africa' (as, indeed, it was) and were positioned some seventy kilometres short of Cairo; the Third Army was totally cut off from its supplies and, were it not for the Security Council and its demand for a ceasefire, doomed. Over 1,000 Egyptian tanks were destroyed; 8,000 Egyptian soldiers were in Israeli prisoner-of-war enclosures (later exchanged for 240 captured Israelis); and the Egyptian dead was estimated at 15,000.

The war neared its end. The Security Council adopted Resolution 383 which called for immediate ceasefire and the implementation of UN Resolution 242, which had been passed after the Six Day War, aimed at establishing 'a just and lasting peace' and 'secure and recognized boundaries for every state in the area', and calling for the 'withdrawal of Israeli armed forces from territories occupied in the conflict'. The new Resolution also required 'negotiations between the parties', a task undertaken by the then US Secretary of State Henry Kissinger, who shuttled back and forth tirelessly between the combatants, eventually negotiating two Israeli-Egyptian 'disengagement' agreements and one between Israel and Syria – all of which involved Israeli relinquishment of some of the territory taken in the Suez region and in the Golan Heights. All told, the talks lasted for a wearying seven and a half months. The impact of the war, and of its implications, on Israel was overwhelming. One important and positive change took place right after the fighting: it was in the relationship between Israel and Egypt; not in the details of the points covered by the final disengagement-of-forces agreement (signed on 11 November 1973 by generals of both countries at Kilometre 101 on the Cairo–Suez road), but in the fact that, for the first time in many years, Israelis and Egyptians sat together, arguing, bargaining and communicating in all but forgotten ways.

For Israel, the winter was truly one of discontent. The mood was sombre, and fateful questions had to be asked – and answered. The sixteen-day war had ended in Israel's victory; the state lived and was intact; but how had it happened? Who was responsible for the lack of awareness, the negligence, the over-confidence and, above all, the deplorable erroneous evaluation of enemy capability and assessment of enemy moves? Why had the Government waited so long before explaining the real situation in those first days? Was enough being done, now that the war was over, to find soldiers missing in

82 Following the ceasefire in the Yom Kippur War, Golda Meir met with Israeli troops on the Golan Heights to answer their many questions. Earlier she had flown south to IDF bases in Egypt for the same purpose.

83 In June 1974 the disengagement agreement between Israel and Syria was concluded (with the aid of US Secretary of State Henry Kissinger) and most Israeli prisoners of war came home.

action, to force the Egyptians and Syrians to give the Red Cross names of captured Israelis, to compel those Governments to permit IDF chaplains to search battlefields for bodies? And even before they were answered, lamely for the most part, the questions toppled heroes from pedestals, undid years of hubris and challenged some of the most sacrosanct of Israeli assumptions.

Golda Meir, Moshe Dayan, even the charismatic Chief of Staff David Elazar, faced an openly hostile public, bent on the pursuit of accountability. Who was to blame? Mrs Meir made no claim to military expertise, but what of her closest advisers: a Chief of Staff and two of his predecessors, both experienced generals, brilliant victors in other wars? The protests, the demands for a Commission of Inquiry, the accusations, were new in Israel's history as was the dominant presence among the demonstrators of reserve officers and distraught, unforgiving parents. At the end of November, the President of the Supreme Court was appointed to head an inquiry commission whose other members included two former Chiefs of Staff (one was Yigael Yadin), another Supreme Court judge and the State Comptroller. On the first day of December, David Ben-Gurion died. For thousands of Israelis, his death at that time of self-examination and doubt was more than an occasion for mourning and eulogy; it was a metaphor for Israel's travail.

The Commission's interim report, published in April 1974, dealt with the state of preparedness. Four high-ranking intelligence officers, among them the head of Military Intelligence, were relieved of their posts; one general was suspended from active service; and the Chief of Staff charged with 'direct responsibility' for what had occurred on the eve of the war, with a recommendation that he relinquish his post – which he immediately did. As for Dayan, 'by standards of reasonable behaviour required ... of the Minister of Defence', he was not found to have been negligent. Golda Meir was similarly cleared. The national frame of mind improved very little in 1974; all winter and deep into spring, IDF reserves were on duty in the south and north; the Israelis captured by the Syrians came home only in June, gaunt and fewer in number than expected; military corteges still wound through the streets as soldiers, their remains recovered from the sands of Sinai, were laid to rest at last.

The war was over, but not violent death. Arab terrorist organizations – headquartered in Lebanon since the 'Black September' of 1970 when the PLO, having disrupted civilian life and threatened government stability, was expelled from Jordan – planned and executed a series of atrocities inside Israel. The favourable prognosis for the success of these operations rested mainly on the seemingly easy job of terrorizing the populations, known to be dissatisfied with their lot, in northern development towns which were also conveniently within easy reach of Lebanon. The initial attack was on Kiryat Shmonah (City of the Eight) founded in 1949 and named for Trumpeldor and the seven comrades who fell with him, in 1920, at nearby Tel Hai. At first glance, it was a logical choice, for Kiryat Shmonah represented an entire range of vulnerabilities. It was intended to be a model metropolis, to serve as a provincial capital for upper Galilee, to be a new town replete with new possibilities for new citizens, most from North Africa, some from Eastern Europe. It was not working out that way; there was not enough housing, capital investment or local skilled labour. To say that influx had outpaced accommodation was to put it mildly, and, in addition, the neighbouring kibbutzim were not helping sufficiently to make the immigrants feel good. By the 1970s, the 15,200 people of Kiryat Shmonah felt themselves to be an illustration of the term 'the Second Israel', just entering common usage. The second Israel connoted chronically jobless fathers unable to cope with the requirements of an impatient, inadequately informed society; overworked, under-educated mothers of huge families, trying to keep house in flats designed for Western couples; children (45 per cent of the town's residents) for whom aggressiveness or apathy tended to substitute for the loss of self-esteem involved in being told so often how backward and useless were the familiar ways of their past, and of their parents. Isolated by geography and circumstances alike, despite all the subsidies and building, Kiryat Shmonah seemed fated never to enter the mainstream of Israeli society, never to catch up.

The testing of the town began after the Six Day War; rockets fired by Arab troops from Lebanon nightly exploded outside houses and on streets, the onslaughts were so severe that a reinforced concrete room was added to each home so that people wouldn't be killed rushing to shelters. The panic on which the PLO had counted did not occur: Kiryat Shmonah stood fast, despite months of bombardment; no one ran away. Then, right after the Yom Kippur War, Kiryat Shmonah became a prime target again. Arab terrorists slipped into town from Lebanon, entered a block of flats, moved from one to another and, in half an hour, killed sixteen civilians — eight of them children. The people of Kiryat Shmonah still stood fast but, this time, were very angry; at the funerals 10,000 men and women sobbed, screamed for revenge and savagely accused the Government of having ignored them. Their terrible rage and their tears got results; not only the Government but also ordinary citizens began to think about the twenty-odd new towns in which conditions were bad, people resentful and development slow, aware now of what had erupted in Kiryat Shmonah and might erupt elsewhere — which it did. Later that year, when Arab terrorists infiltrated Ma'alot, killing a family and twenty school children held as hostages, the fury was almost as explosive. But no one in Ma'alot ran away or asked the Government to retreat from Israel's official decision that there could be no compromise with terrorism.

Ironically enough the one event of that period which filled Israelis with elation also had to with terrorism. It was the astonishing rescue of passengers and crew members of a French aeroplane hijacked on 27 June 1976 on its way from Athens to Paris (the flight having originated in Tel Aviv), taken to Uganda and plucked from captivity there on 4 July by Israeli commandos. The audacity and drama of the now-legendary airborne strike, across some 2,500 miles, were spectacular proof that international terrorism could be stopped in its tracks — if the will and the need were there. The Arab hijackers (led by two Germans) belonged to the same PLO-affiliated organization, the Popular Front for the Liberation of Palestine, as the attackers of Kiryat Shmonah, Ma'alot and other infiltrated Israeli towns and villages. Since the hijacking was partly sponsored by Libya, the stolen plane was allowed to land in that country before flying on to Uganda's Entebbe airport, where 256 frightened passengers and twelve members of the crew were kept under guard. The price set for their release included freeing fifty-three convicted terrorists held in Israel and elsewhere, a ransom that would, however reluctantly, have been paid to save so many threatened lives — the terrorists having announced that, if turned down, they would blow up the airport — but for one major, and telling, error of the hijackers judgment, 'a development', to quote Chaim Herzog, then Israel's Ambassador to the UN (in 1986 he became the state's sixth President), at the Security Council a week later, 'so sinister and so pregnant with memories of the past that no member of the Jewish people ... could fail to recall its horrible significance'.

In the course of the first days of their incarceration inside Entebbe airport, most of the passengers were, in fact, released — except for the eighty-three Jewish men, women and children earlier separated from the rest. 'When this ominous reminiscent selection began ... it became apparent to the Government of Israel,' Herzog declared, 'that there was no alternative other than to conduct ... an operation to save the lives of its citizens.'

The meticulously co-ordinated preparations for the military option —

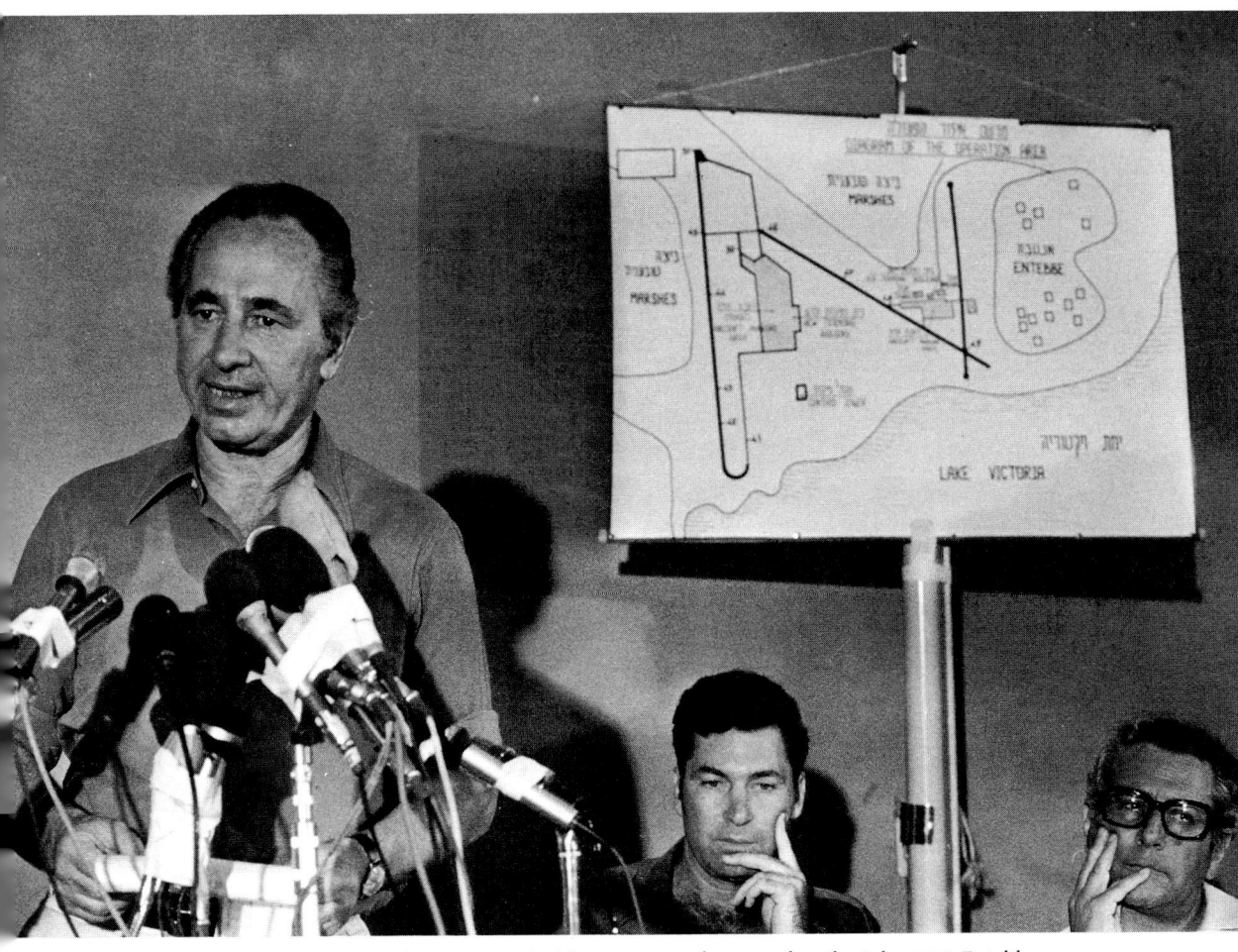

84 Defence Minister Shimon Peres holds a press conference after the July 1976 Entebbe rescue operation. On his left, General Dan Shomron.

approved by Prime Minister Yitzhak Rabin, Defence Minister Shimon Peres and Opposition Leader Menachem Begin — were based on secrecy, speed and, above all, surprise. They involved such dicey projects as the discreet activation of Israeli contacts in Kenya — which, in common with many other African states, had broken diplomatic relations with Israel in 1973 (but none the less allowed the Entebbe-bound plane not only to overfly Kenya but also to be given landing and service facilities there), the expert cautious questioning of freed hostages; mock assaults carried out in the heart of the desert; and the skilful feeding of 'disinformation' through 'channels' to the terrorists and Uganda's irrational dictator President Idi Amin, who were persuaded that their conditions would shortly be met. The operation, carried out with split-second timing, was led by General Dan Shomron (since April 1987 Israeli's Chief of Staff), the attack on the airport by its only Israeli military fatality, Lieutenant-Colonel Jonathan Netanyahu; three hostages were killed, several Israeli soldiers badly wounded, and one elderly Jewish lady passenger, taken from the airport to hospital in Kampala, was never seen or heard from again. But the raiding party of giant Hercules transport planes and Boeing 707s, which, in a total of ninety minutes on Uganda's soil, lifted nearly a hundred Jews out of mortal peril, did wonders not only for those whom it delivered but also for Israel's overall state of mind.

CHAPTER 9

Begin, Sadat and the Peace Treaty

The 'upheaval', or 'shake-up' is the way all Israelis, regardless of political persuasion, to this day describe the result of the May 1977 national elections which brought to power – for the first time since the establishment of the state – a Likud ('unity')-led Government, headed by Menachem Begin, long-time leader of the right-wing Herut Party. Accompanied by the qualms, apprehensions and, in many cases, nightmares of a Labour movement profoundly jarred by its defeat after twenty-nine years of virtually absolute control, Begin's tenure began as a considerable success. Unbending on the future of the West Bank (now officially, and biblically, referred to as Judea and Samaria), which he regarded as integral to the Land of Israel and vital to security, he was more elastic in his public utterances on Sinai and the Golan Heights. Begin's cabinet contained some new faces but was made up also of familiar, if unexpected, ones, the appointment of Labourite Moshe Dayan as Foreign Minister being the first bombshell. Announced on late-night television, it upset armies of applecarts, including those of his erstwhile comrades who, from then on, viewed Dayan as a traitor to Socialism, to the Labour Alignment and to peace; and of key Likud supporters, who had blithely taken it for granted that this important Ministry would go to one of the faithful. The Defence Ministry went to Ezer Weizman (Chaim Weizmann's nephew), a dashing ex-RAF pilot who had headed Israel's air force, was a former brother-in-law of Dayan and a darling both of Herut and of the Israeli press. Another appointment was of David Levy, one-time building worker, father of eleven children, a resident of the Jordan Valley development town of Beit Shean, whose cabinet position (Minister of Construction, Housing and Immigration) particularly gratified Israel's significant Moroccan community. The later naming of Yigael Yadin (founder of the new liberal Democratic Movement for Change) as Deputy Prime Minister, and the invitation to Israel's always controversial General Ariel Sharon — in private life a highly innovative farmer, in public life the moving spirit behind the creation of the Likud bloc — to serve as Minister of Agriculture, were equally attention-getting. Whatever else they were or were not, the 'new boys' were colourful, talented and experienced in their respective fields, something that further salted Labour Alignment wounds.

Menachem Begin, a Knesset oppositionist since the start of Israel's parliamentary life, was born in 1913 in Brest Litovsk (then part of Lithuania, today part of the Belorussian Soviet Republic), graduated from Warsaw University, became a devout lifelong disciple of Vladimir Jabotinsky, an active member of Jabotinsky's Revisionist Party and a major figure in the Betar youth organization which inculcated tens of thousands of young East European Jews with a fiery, semi-militaristic love of Zion.

When the Nazis occupied Poland in 1939, Begin fled to Lithuania, where he was arrested by the Soviet authorities and sentenced to hard labour in a Siberian gulag. Freed in 1942 to join the war against Germany, he found his way to Palestine, became commander of the Irgun Zvai Leumi and, a much-wanted, never-caught man, directed the IZL's underground battle against the British. In 1948, he founded the Herut Party and in May 1967, when a Government of National Unity was formed just prior to the Six Day War, he became Minister without Portfolio. Three years later, he took himself and his Party out of the Government when a majority, led by Prime Minister Golda Meir, accepted a US initiative for peace talks with the Arabs (authored by Secretary of State William Rogers) which implied, Herut believed, negotiating withdrawal from the administered territories before there was peace. Known for the formality, even elegance, of his clothes (he was never seen tieless or without a jacket), speech and manners, Begin was also considered by his adoring followers to be a great orator, though other Israelis abhorred his full-blown rhetoric. Everyone, however, agreed that he was a man of complete probity, of superior intelligence and of infinite dedication.

Labour's diminished support did more than hand the heavy responsibility for governing Israel to a new cast working under a new director, more than simply punish those whose long record had been badly blemished, and possibly typified, by the sort of over-confidence that, in the eyes of most voters, was responsible for the initial set-backs of the Yom Kippur War. Beyond these, the transfer of power expressed a deep-seated desire for political change as such. By achieving this change, however traumatically, the Israeli electorate corrected an anomaly which, once dealt with, was unlikely to recur: the permanent rule of one party.

The acute antagonism between Labour (in its various combinations and permutations) and Herut, largest and most dominant component of the Likud, had its origins in the clash of ideologies, temperaments and vision which, in the pre-state 1930s, already led Jabotinsky to withdraw his faction from the World Zionist Organization and set in motion a rival organization headed by himself. Mutual hostility and disapproval flared periodically, turning into something akin to hatred in June 1933 when Chaim Arlosoroff, a brilliant young Labour leader, was assassinated by unknown assailants as he strolled one evening on the Tel Aviv beach with his wife. Three members of the Revisionist Party were charged with his murder but eventually acquitted. None the less, the Labour movement, bereft of a favourite son, responded to Arlosoroff's tragic death (and to the acquittals) with fury, continuing to denounce Revisionism as fascist and, from then on, to give Revisionists and their political heirs, first members of the Irgun Zvai Leumi, later of Herut, very short shrift – something which, for a party that seemed immutably enthroned, was not difficult.

At various junctures in the past, the exigencies of the Yishuv's struggle against the British forced tenuous reconciliation between Left and Right, between the dissident Irgun Zvai Leumi headed by Begin and the Haganah, politically directed by Ben-Gurion. But for the most part, the relationship remained almost as virulent as on 22 June 1948 (during the first truce of the War of Independence) when Ben-Gurion ordered the sinking of the ss *Altalena*, an Irgun ship loaded with much-needed arms which the IZL refused to turn over unconditionally to the newly formed Israel Defence Forces. 'There are not going to be two states and there are not going to be two armies,' Ben-Gurion had thundered. Refusing to abandon the smoking ship, until the very last minute before it went under, Begin could hardly have imagined that just under three decades later, he would become Israel's sixth Prime Minister.

Undeniably the under-dog for years, Herut increasingly attracted supporters from the ranks of the so-called Second Israel, people who identified themselves with it as equally deprived and discriminated-against and who were eager to oust the gods that had failed them. The crowds that surrounded Begin at every opportunity, chanting his name and extolling his virtues, acclaimed him as their champion, the one man who – unlike anybody in the Labour hierarchy, they insisted – would see to it that they received their fair

85 Menachem Begin refused to leave the burning *Altalena* until the wounded were evacuated. Then he descended, was picked up by a flat-bottomed boat and rowed to shore. That night he spoke for two hours on the Irgun radio station – and Israelis flocked to the beach to see the ship.

share of the national cake, however austere the ingredients might be.

The pipe of peace had been offered around by Israelis for decades; the list of dates, meetings, sites and participants in the succession of clandestine, always abortive rendezvous with Arabs of consequence (or their chosen intermediaries), not, by any standards, a short one. It was not until 1977 and the various Israeli-Egyptian separation-of-forces agreements which followed the Yom Kippur War, that any Arab country agreed to enter into a contractual commitment to forgo the military option in the dispute with Israel. That this happened is due, to an impressive degree, to the far-sightedness, hard-headedness, tenacity and religious faith of the three men – US President Jimmy Carter, Egypt's President Anwar Sadat and Israel's Premier Menachem Begin – whose names are linked in perpetuity with the treaty and its final signature, on the North Lawn of the White House, on 26 March 1978. In fact, it is probable that, had any one of these driven personalities given up at any point in the tortuous sixteen months of negotiation, the treaty would not have come into existence. But all three, though they had little in common personally, were alike in their deep conviction of the need to bring to an end the state of war between Israel and the largest, most powerful, most amenable of the Arab states. It is perhaps instructive for crystal-ball-gazers that the supposedly inflexible and fanatical Begin was the Israeli statesman who, when he felt sure that it had to be done, traded territory for political concessions – as an act of faith.

In June 1977, President Carter cabled the usual post-election congratulations to Prime Minister Begin: 'The important part of the signal, however, was not the polite goodwill message,' wrote Moshe Dayan, himself soon to be an indispensable Israeli negotiator, 'but a practical appeal to Begin to start peace negotiations with the Arabs.' The appeal was accompanied by an invitation to Washington where, in July, Begin explained to Carter that Israel was ready to make 'a significant withdrawal' of forces in Sinai and, although staying in the Golan Heights, to redeploy to a more permanent boundary; as for Judea, Samaria and the Gaza Strip, Israel would not permit the transfer of these to 'any foreign sovereign authority', but, on the other hand, did not demand *Israeli* sovereignty. Moreover, Israel was prepared to start talks without any preconditions and would accept Resolutions 383 and 242 as a basis for such parleys. All summer, men bent on peace travelled on its urgent behalf: Begin paid a call on Romania's Nicolae Ceausescu; so did Sadat, wanting to know how tough Begin was and whether he was really on the level about wanting a solution. The US Secretary of State met with leaders of almost all the Middle Eastern countries, telling each one to get down to brass tacks and do so quickly; Moshe Dayan, heavily and uncomfortably disguised ('on my skull the mane of a beatnik'), visited Hassan, King of Morocco, three times and talked in depth with the Egyptian Deputy Premier, with Jordan's King Hussein and with President Carter. It began to look as though there might be accord on three principles: no more wars between Egypt and Israel; the formal restoration of Egyptian sovereignty over Sinai; and the demilitarization of most of the Peninsula.

At the beginning of November, addressing the Egyptian parliament, President Sadat made the first move. Departing from his prepared text, he announced: 'The Israelis are going to be very surprised on hearing this. I am ready to meet them in their home.... I am ready to go to the Knesset to discuss peace with them, if need be.' Two days later, in a message broadcast to the Egyptian people, Menachem Begin took up the initiative: 'It will be a pleasure to welcome your President with the traditional hospitality you and we have inherited from our common father Abraham....' Dated 15 November 1977, Begin's official invitation to the President of Egypt, handed to the US Ambassador to Israel to pass on, ended with the phrase: 'May I assure you that the parliament, the Government and the people of Israel will receive you with respect and cordiality.'

Both host and guest had notifications to make: Begin informed the Knesset that such a letter was *en route* to Cairo; Sadat flew to Damascus to talk to Syrian President Hafez Assad. On 17 November, Jerusalem and Cairo announced that Sadat's visit to the Jewish state would start on Saturday 19 November after the end of the Sabbath. The excitement was laced with worry. What if Sadat did not turn up? His Foreign Minister had resigned on hearing the news, and there were reports of overall mounting Egyptian opposition. What if Assad voiced strong objections? What if something happened to Sadat in the course of his visit to Israel? Some 2,000 representatives of the media had already arrived in the country. What would they witness? Nor did anyone forget, even in the tension and astonishment, that this was not the first time that Sadat had taken Israel by surprise! But at 8 p.m. sharp, on the evening of 20 November 1977, all the uncertainty notwithstanding, the first head of an Arab state ever to visit Israel stood smiling at the door of Egypt's Number One aeroplane which had just landed at Ben-Gurion airport.

There was a red-carpet welcome: the Israel Defence Forces band played the Egyptian anthem; there were fanfares of trumpets and a twenty-one-gun salute; at the plane were the President and the Prime Minister of Israel; and there was a receiving line which included Israel's Chief Rabbis, cabinet members, Golda Meir, the Chief of Staff, Arab leaders from the West Bank and – theirs the only unsmiling faces in the rejoicing crowd – the top security teams of Israel and Egypt. The improbable dream had come true. In thousands upon thousands of Israeli homes, families crowded round television sets, the eyes of adults bulging at the wonder of seeing an Arab ruler inspect units of the IDF, Egyptian flags flying everywhere, Arabic banner headlines ('*Ahlan wa Sahlan*, Welcome to President Sadat') in the extra editions of all papers and at the small hard-to-believe exchanges: Sadat asking whether Ariel Sharon was at the airport, then nodding at the ex-general who had led the Israeli counter-attack across the Suez Canal in the Yom Kippur War – 'I wanted to catch you there!' 'I am glad to have you here, Mr President,' Sharon answered; Sadat beaming as he shook hands with Moshe Dayan – 'Don't worry, Moshe, it will be all right.'

The risk Sadat was running was, as the *Jerusalem Post* editorial had it, 'patently enormous ... whatever else may be said of the Egyptian President, he is not lacking in the courage of his convictions'. The salient facts of Sadat's life bore out the assertion. Born in 1918 in a Nile Delta village – his father Egyptian, his mother Sudanese – a German sympathizer in World War II, he was one of the officers who helped overthrow the corrupt Egyptian monarchy in 1952. Eventually named by Nasser as Vice President, Sadat succeeded him when Nasser died in 1970. Never credited by his opponents as being either strong or especially capable, by 1971 – already quite adept at hurling bolts from the blue – Sadat had flung into jail all those who plotted against him and firmly ensconced himself in the seat of power. By 1972, again with no warning, he threw out of Egypt the 20,000 Soviet military advisers who had built up the Egyptian army, and thus launched the Egyptian shift away from the Soviet Union, severing the connection begun by Nasser and paving the way for close US ties.

In Jerusalem, pomp and protocol marked every ceremonial stage of the visit, and nothing that was done or said was less than amazing: Sadat laid a wreath at the eternal flame for Israeli war dead; prayed at the Al Aksa mosque in the Old City; ecumenically visited the Holy Sepulchre; toured Yad Vashem; met with Labour Alignment Members of Knesset (including its affiliated Arab list); nibbled at huge chocolate sponge pyramids connected by a chocolate bridge with 'Peace' written on it in whipped cream; waved warmly at children wearing T-shirts adorned by portraits of Begin and himself and the appropriate advice ('all you need is love'); and jested with Golda Meir ('It must go on, face-to-face, between us so that even an old lady like myself ... I *know* that is what you always called me Mr President! ... will live to see the day of peace!'). An Egyptian pressman sumed it up aptly: 'Suddenly, black has become white.'

Sadat's speech at the Knesset, which lasted fifty-five minutes, was made in Arabic. Reviewing the past, he stressed that he had not come to make any separate agreement between Egypt and Israel nor 'to seek a partial peace.... I have come so that together we can build a durable peace based on justice.... In all sincerity, I tell you ... and I declare it to the whole world, we accept living with you in permanent peace based on justice ... there was a huge wall between us which you tried to build up over a quarter of a century but was destroyed in 1973.' He called for complete withdrawal from the Arab territories occupied in 1967, terming this a 'foregone conclusion not open to discussion or debate' and for 'achievement of the fundamental rights of the Palestinian people ... including the right to establish their own state'; and for 'ending the state of belligerency in the region'. Begin's Hebrew speech, lasting forty minutes, included an invitation to the President of Syria and to King Hussein to follow in Sadat's footsteps. 'Our country is open', he said, 'to the citizens of Egypt, and I make no conditions on our part for this statement.' He appealed for negotiations, proposing, 'in the name of the great majority of the members of this parliament', that no side should present prior conditions, and ended with the hope that 'we may reach the day we yearn for ... the day of peace; for ... so the Psalmist of Israel said: "Justice and peace have kissed."'

Nothing, and everything, had changed. Both addresses were somewhat anti-climactic; Sadat had made no major concessions. 'The October war was the last war,' he said repeatedly, but also he reiterated that the issue of withdrawal as a principle was not negotiable. As he left Israel, Sadat again emphasized that the Arabs could not accept less than complete Israeli withdrawal from lands taken in 1967; a state of war still existed. On Monday 21 November, the whirlwind visit was over. In a farewell meeting with the press, Sadat made clear that, from then on, everything depended on Begin. 'There is need,' he said, 'for ... drastic decisions. I have already taken my share.... I shall be waiting for those decisions of Premier Begin and the Knesset.'

86 In 1987, on the tenth anniversary of Sadat's visit to Jerusalem (above), all the still amazing details were vividly relived by the Israeli public and press.

'The dialogue started... the precise modalities are still to be established,' editorialized that day's *Jerusalem Post*. Establishing these modalities turned out to be precarious, time-consuming, frequently thwarting for all concerned. Searching for a way of describing the shared Israeli feeling of let-down as the Egyptians departed – though their leaving was as red-carpeted as their arrival – the *Post*'s cartoonist hit on the wry phrase, 'post-Sadatal depression'. In the event, it was not inaccurate.

In December 1977, Begin made his first visit to Egypt, to Ismailia. The atmosphere was restrained: there were no Israeli flags and no Egyptian military band; the leaders talked, for the most part each saying only what the other already knew; Sadat's demand for Israel's complete and abiding withdrawal from the West Bank colliding – as was obvious it would – with Begin's adamant refusal to consider the final surrender to anyone of a single inch of the Land. The solution, if there was one, had to lie in the extremely narrow space that might be created between the two basically conflicting approaches. Hence the Israeli suggestions of 'administrative autonomy' for the West Bank – with Israel in charge of security and Israelis free to settle in those territories – perhaps to be reviewed within five years; and of a phased withdrawal from Sinai that would leave Israeli settlements there intact and under Israel's protection. They were flatly turned down. Still, however disappointing Begin's trip, at least the talks were not ended; working committees were established and meetings set for the beginning of 1978. But ill-luck (if not ill-will), mutual suspicion and misunderstanding dogged the negotiations. Within hours, members of the Egyptian working committee were called home.

To the Israelis involved in the talks, it was as though no one remembered that the 1967 war had been defensive, as though Jordanian control of the West Bank went without saying, as though Israel and its Prime Minister were unwilling to meet Sadat even halfway. Frustrated by the bogging-down of an initiative which held profound implications for his country, and for himself, President Carter, placing the full weight of his immense prestige in the balance, proving himself no less stubborn than Sadat or Begin and almost as vitally concerned with peace in the Middle East, issued an invitation for September 1978 that could not be refused: he summoned Begin, Sadat and their respective advisers to a 'summit conference' at Camp David, the official US presidential retreat in Maryland, where everyone would stay until the

87 Prime Minister Begin, President Sadat, the then Speaker of the Knesset (later Israel's Prime Minister) Yitzhak Shamir, and Israel's President Ephraim Katzir at the Knesset, November 1977.

88 Prime Minister Begin's visit to Sadat in Ismailia, December 1977, was distinctly low-key, minus Israeli flags or a band. Behind Begin is Moshe Dayan, a principal Israeli negotiator.

talks bore fruit — a matter, so the White House initially believed, of merely a few days.

Later President Carter wrote: 'Sadat seems to trust me too much; Begin not enough.' His own visible preference for Sadat was based, to some extent, on his perception of Sadat in the continuing role of a leader boldly intent on securing peace while Begin, pedantically and obstinately, concerned himself with formulations and legalistics. To Israel's Prime Minister, it looked otherwise. The plan Sadat brought to Camp David included all-too-familiar demands plus new and daunting ones: i.e. that Israel compensate Egypt for damage caused to the Egyptian civilian population; that Israel indemnify Egypt for the oil taken from Sinai since 1967; and that Israel withdraw from East Jerusalem to the city's 1949 lines, which was, of course, entirely unacceptable to Begin. As the arguments and counter-arguments were volleyed back and forth, without results, Carter decided to take over. To avoid deadlock, he set a deadline; saw to it that, gradually, Sadat got most of what mattered to Egypt; and forced the production of one framework for an Israel–Egypt peace treaty and a wider one for peace in the Middle East. Camp David may have been a playground for US Chiefs of State, but it was not that — despite the informality, the scenery and the limitless American hospitality — for Menachem Begin and the Israelis who accompanied him there for thirteen fateful days. Nor did the chemistry between Begin and Sadat improve. When both were awarded the 1978 Nobel Peace Prize, certainly an occasion for *rapprochement* between them, Sadat, now the object of violent criticism throughout the Arab Middle East, opted not to highlight the new relationship with Israel and stayed at home; Begin had to accept the honour alone.

By March 1979, Carter was impatient. He had staked a great deal on the treaty and wanted it signed. Only his presence, his goading, his denial of the possibility that the gamble for peace might be lost, could ensure completion of the arduous and nerve-wracking bargaining. He flew to Cairo, on to Israel where he addressed a special session of the Knesset, returned to Cairo and at last left with the package he wanted. The main points of the treaty concerned total withdrawal from Sinai (over a three-year period); agreed security arrangements on both sides of the Egyptian-Israeli border; the establishment of peace with 'normal and friendly relations' in various fields, including exchange of ambassadors; free passage through the Suez Canal for Israeli ships and cargoes; permission for Israel to buy oil, 'under normal commercial terms' from the Sinai fields being returned; and agreement that negotiations begin 'for putting into effect the Camp David agreement on Palestinian self-rule on the West Bank and in the Gaza Strip'.

The Preamble, noting that the framework was intended to constitute a basis for peace between 'Israel and each of the other Arab neighbours prepared to negotiate peace with it...', invited these 'other Arab Parties' to join the peace process with Israel. A letter to Carter, signed by Begin and Sadat and dated 26 March, specifically inviting King Hussein to join the negotiations concerning the West Bank and the Gaza Strip, was among the various treaty texts. So was an explanatory note by Carter to the effect that 'the expression "West Bank" is understood by the Government of Israel to mean "Judea and Samaria".'

At the treaty-signing ceremony, all three statesmen referred to the words of the Prophet Isaiah (2:4): 'and they shall beat their swords into plowshares, and their spears into pruning hooks: nation shall not lift up sword against nation, neither shall they learn war any more.' Jimmy Carter briefly quoted the Koran; Begin spoke of the Holocaust and read Psalm 126 ('we were like them that dream'); and Sadat talked of the liberation of Arab land and 'the reinstitution of Arab authority' in the administered territories. It was a great day all right but even in Israel, wrote the *New York Times*, 'there was none of the euphoria that swept the country ... when Sadat visited Jerusalem'. Instead, there was apprehension about the yielding of so much that Israel had developed in Sinai, from airfields to the new model town of Yamit, from road networks to thriving resorts – and the miles of land that gave a sense of security. Even President Yitzhak Navon spoke, on 26 March, with concern about vital territory and installations ceded. What indeed lay ahead in the West Bank and the Gaza Strip? Might not the treaty trigger a chain reaction culminating in a Palestinian state on Israel's eastern border? Was not Sinai too heavy a price for the victors to pay for 'no more war'? Questions filled the air but there were no sure answers; nor did a word of praise for Sadat, or of relief at the prospect of peace, come from a single Arab state.

It is said that only Begin could have brought off the Sinai withdrawal and made that most painful of all concessions: the evacuation of the Israeli settlements in northern Sinai. Everything possible had been done to reverse the decision, all available strings pulled, all feasible appeals made, all existing loopholes re-examined in the fading hope that the Yamit district and the pretty town that was its centrepiece might be kept by Israel without shattering

89 Begin, Sadat and US President Jimmy Carter sign the peace treaty between Israel and Egypt on the lawn of the White House, Washington DC, 26 March 1979.

the fragile working-out of peace with Egypt. But nothing availed. Sadly, quietly, efficiently the people of Yamit got ready to leave for good; financially compensated for material loss, they solaced each other with the knowledge that they were part of a pact which would alter the way things were in the Middle East, and some, hoping that the treaty would truly unite two nations, opted to relocate just across the border.

But it was not to be so smooth: ultra-nationalistic volunteers from the young settlements of Judea and Samaria of which Mr Begin and Herut were so proud, hardliners come to Sinai to protest and resist, took over the empty houses and refused to budge. The final evacuation, which started on 23 April 1982, became disorderly; the squatters had to be dragged away, pushed into pens and sprayed with foam, while Israeli soldiers systematically reduced Yamit to rubble, obliterating close to a decade of Israeli presence in the area, well aware that what they were doing might change their lives and Israel's history. By midnight, 25 April, the whole of Sinai was in Egyptian hands, the Israeli villages razed, the blue-and-white flag lowered at Ophira (better known as Sharm el-Sheikh), and only a tiny area, Taba, right on the frontier, still in dispute. The last Israeli was gone from the Peninsula as had been pledged, only free to return when equipped with a visa.

Sadat died before Yamit, killed in Cairo in October 1981 by a Moslem fanatic, his death also, perhaps, part of the cost of a most expensive peace.

No one knew then, not even the crystal ball-gazers, that the memory of Yamit would recede, within weeks, in the face of the heartbreaking reality of yet another war from another direction altogether, nor that the peace treaty, so laboriously gestated, would survive the blood-letting in Lebanon and, after that, Begin's own withdrawal. Promises exchanged in Jerusalem, Cairo, Washington and Camp David were kept, in the main – though the relationship was notably cool insofar as Egypt was concerned and the enthusiastic traffic almost entirely one way.

90 New settlements sprouted throughout Judea and Samaria in the 1970s. One such pioneering community is Ma'aleh Efraim in eastern Samaria.

91 The forcible evacuation of Yamit was carried out on schedule despite the financial and emotional price tag. Altogether eighteen Israeli settlements were evacuated in Sinai, all on time, mostly after only token clashes with the army, April 1982.

92 Opposite: The Israeli flag lowered at Sharm el-Sheikh, administered and developed by Israel since 1967 and handed over to Egypt in April 1982. With it went the Israeli presence in Sinai.

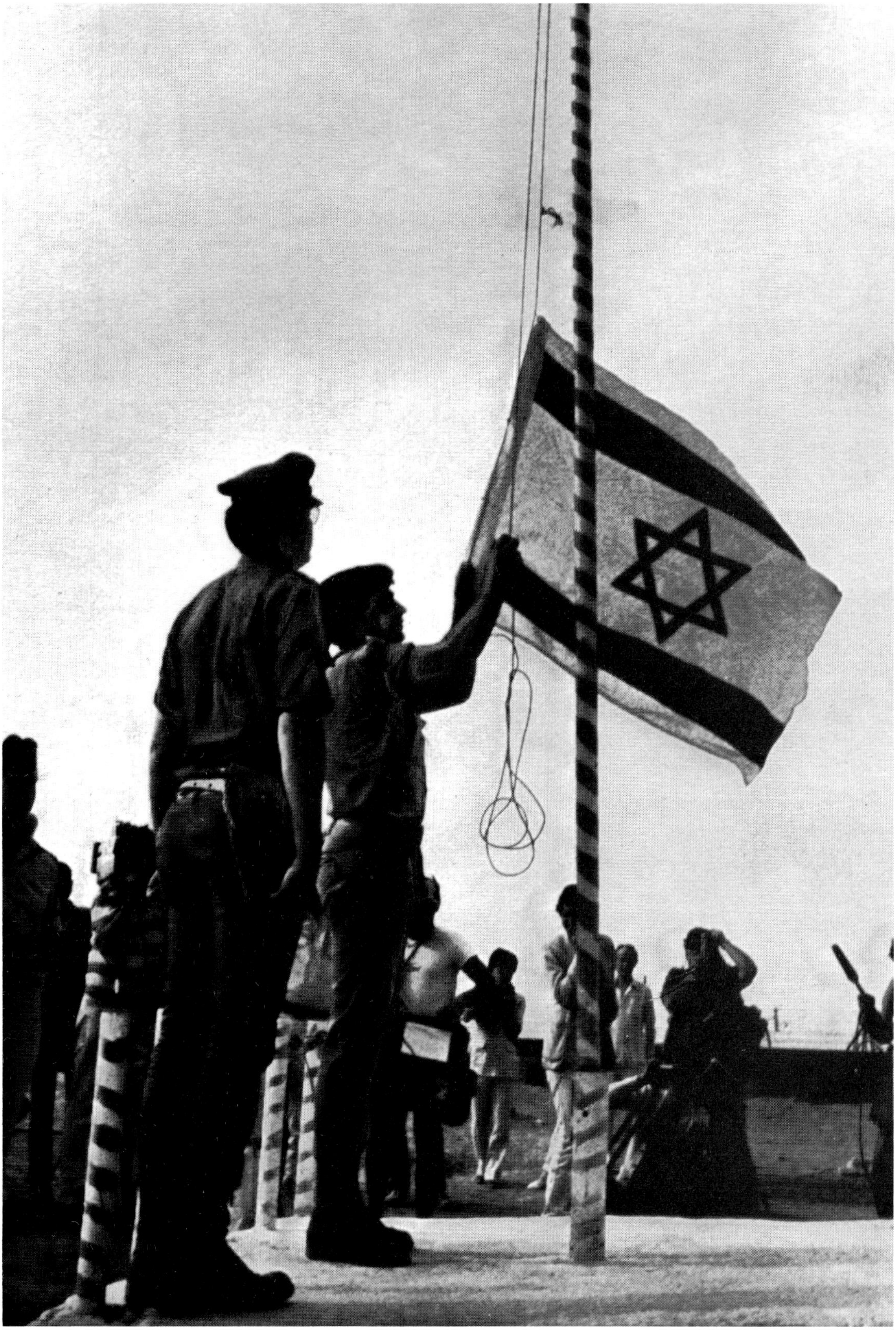

CHAPTER 10

Israel at Forty

In the spring of 1988, Israel turned forty. Not a great age for a state, least of all one with the millennia-long sweep of Jewish history behind it. The density and tempo of events, the hazards, elations, disputes of those two-score years – though they made for alterations in the self-image and world view of many Israelis – left intact continuing consensus regarding the state's primary role as Ingatherer of the Exiles. Although the Jewish masses of the world seemed not to perceive of the National Home as being, in any literal sense, *their* home, immigration never stopped. There were slack times when few immigrants came and many Israelis left; in the main, those Jews who wanted to settle in Israel could not; those who were able to did not. But there was never a time throughout the forty years that, from somewhere or other, newly arrived Jews were not in the process of becoming permanent residents of the Land. In the 1980s, two very different groups of immigrants, men, women and children from opposite ends of the earth who represented cultures separated by thousands of years – the Jews of the Soviet Union and those of Ethiopia – were the centre of national attention in this regard.

The struggle of Soviet Jews for religious and cultural freedom, for the right to live fully as Jews, to pass on to their children the traditions of Judaism and to do so, if they wished, in the Jewish state, stirred public opinion in the West as few such sagas have done. From the 1960s on, when details of the deteriorating, increasingly dangerous situation of the activist elements in the two million-strong Jewish population of the USSR leaked out and became widely known, the response abroad was enormous. Under the relentless pressure of organizations specifically founded (in Europe, North and South America and Israel) to try to force the Soviets to let the Jews go, faced by the forceful intercession of foreign heads of state, parliaments and ranking personalities, the Soviet Union – despite anti-Semitism and the extreme harshness with which it punished those who repeatedly applied for permission to leave — finally permitted a very limited degree of emigration. By 1987, a total of about 260,000 to 280,000 Jews departed the Soviet Union for Israel; some 160,000 to 180,000 actually settled there, the rest opting for Canada and the US.

Like all campaigns, this one too has had its heroes, its triumphs, its losses and its casualties. Most of the Soviet *émigrés* arriving at Ben-Gurion airport are so-called *refuseniks*, brave, unbreakable people whose requests had been turned down, whose jobs were taken away from them, who had served Siberian prison terms under close-to-unendurable conditions, but who had been sustained by optimism, courage and the knowledge that their wives, mothers and friends overseas were clamouring for their release — hunger-striking, pleading, marching, serving as inspiration for hundreds of thousands of volunteers everywhere. For those caught up in the cause, and especially for Israelis, two young Russian Jews, Anatoly and Avital Shcharansky, embodied the fight for freedom: Avital, granted the yearned-for exit permit in 1974, ordered to leave the USSR forthwith, hastily married Anatoly and then — modestly, indefatigably, effectively — over the next twelve years publicly protested his nine-year imprisonment, the brutality of the work camps in which he was incarcerated, and their long separation, and called on captains and kings for his release; Anatoly himself, in the spring of 1986 upon his eventual joyous arrival in Israel, became the instantly impressive spokesman for those left behind in Russia, a personification of the qualities needed to come through intact. The Shcharanskys' suffering, valour and love for each other, the baby girl born to them in Jerusalem, made them irresistible to the media, proof that not only fairy-tales have happy endings but that there were real grounds for the hope that, one day, the Soviet Government would indeed fling open those gates.

Soviet Jews were entering Israel in trickles, sometimes a number of families at once, sometimes an individual or two, occasionally a few hundred people a month. Not so the Ethiopian Jews, 7,000 of whom were brought to Israel within one year, arriving from the end of 1984 to the end of 1985 in 'Operation Moses' airlifts organized in response to desperate conditions of drought, disease and famine prevailing throughout that part of Africa. They were not, however, the first nor, it was hoped, the last Ethiopian immigrants to the Land. Almost the same number had arrived in the country between 1980 and the autumn of 1984, with possibly 2,000 more having perished in the attempt to reach refugee camps in the Sudan. Accurate figures

93 The US Ambassador to West Germany escorting Anatoly (now Natan) Shcharansky across the bridge to West Germany on his way to Israel, February 1986.

were lacking, but another 6,000 or 7,000 Jews may still be in Ethiopia, members of a unique community considered by some scholars to have descended from the Jews who lived there in antiquity, intermarrying with converts from the local population – an explanation that accounts for the dark-skinned, black-eyed, non-Semitic good looks of Ethiopian Jewry. A less scholarly, if more romantic, version has it that they are direct descendants of those Jews who accompanied Menelek (the son of King Solomon and the Queen of Sheba) from Jerusalem to Ethiopia after the Red Sea Queen's famous visit over 2,000 years ago.

Most Ethiopian Israelis are young, many in Israel without their families, their adjustment slow, even painful; no single aspect of the state, or Western life, is initially familiar to them, beginning with the way people dress and on through to the way things are measured. Worst of all has been the humiliation of rabbinical debates as to what kind of Jews they really are and whether or not their Orthodox conversion should be required. Out of their bewilderment and dissatisfaction have come recent demands that they be united with their families again, that Israel bring to its shores the rest of the community. The Soviet Government has, at least, shown itself somewhat sensitive to world opinion; not so, thus far, the Government of Ethiopia, its ban on Jewish emigration still complete. In the meantime, a public opinion poll conducted in Israel in the second half of 1987 revealed that immigration remains a top national priority, seen by the overwhelming majority of Israelis as worth whatever further sharings and sacrifices may be involved.

Although its long-term physical and political survival is still regarded by its more determined enemies as uncertain, its priorities and much of its collective behaviour still profoundly influenced by military needs, and its victories in battle still the protective parentheses within which the State of Israel develops, each of the wars fought since 1948 has been subjected to critical analysis by a citizenry that hungers for the fruits of peace and, as in the case of Lebanon in 1982, is prepared to take up arms with this one trophy in mind.

Up to 1969–70, Israel's border with Lebanon was quiet, the armistice agreement of 1949 that fixed the international boundary rarely violated. Even during the Six Day War of 1967, Lebanon did not engage in any military action against Israel. But when the Palestinian terrorists, thrown out of Jordan by King Hussein, began to crowd into Lebanon, turning that country, most especially the south, into their operational centre, the days of this once prosperous centre of world trade and tourism were numbered, Lebanon's doom was sealed and Israel's north seriously threatened. The complexity and fragility of the Lebanese situation were considerable: a weak government nervously trying to rule a population of three million which included one and a quarter million Christians (known as Maronites), nearly a million and a half Moslems divided into two antagonistic groups (the Shi'ites and the Sunnis), 200,000 Druze and about 30,000 Arab refugees living there since 1948. At best, it was potentially a most explosive mix.

The money and arms so liberally donated by Syria and Saudi Arabia to the Palestine Liberation Organization flexed PLO muscles in a way which badly upset the Syrians, who then also moved in. The result was seven years of civil war. The central authority of the Lebanese Government disintegrated: the PLO, leftist forces, the Syrian army and the Christian militias all strove to gain control. Thousands died; Beirut was largely destroyed; the PLO finally attained almost total dominance in the south, now both a springboard for attack on Israel's northern settlements and training ground for international terrorist movements. The south, however, was also where a small group of Maronites were managing to withstand PLO assaults in an enclave of about 120 square miles which they called 'Free Lebanon'. Headed by an officer from the Lebanese army, Major Saad Hadad, this south Lebanese force was encouraged and supported by Israel, which also maintained, throughout the civil war and after it, an opening (known as 'The Good Fence') in the border where medical aid, food, fuel and advice for farmers were provided for the roughly 100,000 Moslem and Christian Lebanese in the area. Whenever the PLO struck hard, Israel retaliated. In 1978, a large-scale IDF operation was mounted to push the PLO back; after two months Israel withdrew voluntarily and UN forces entered the region. But the attacks on civilians in Israel's north went on. In 1981, President Ronald Reagan sent an envoy to the Middle East; a ceasefire was negotiated but was constantly violated, while the Soviets sent off a supply of weapons to the PLO which would have sufficed to arm five infantry brigades, a build-up that even the presence of 7,000 UN troops did not stop. The stockpiling had only one purpose and its message was unmistakable.

By then, for ordinary people in much of northern Israel, especially in vulnerable places like Kiryat Shmonah, the incessant bombardments from Lebanon were making life hell. That year, Israeli elections took place, once again the Likud emerging triumphant. Newly appointed Defence Minister Ariel Sharon and Chief of Staff Rafael Eitan were of the opinion that the time had come, at long last, to eradicate the PLO's menacing power base in

94 Ethiopian Jews encounter friends and relatives at the Western Wall.

Lebanon. The overall stated aim of the action which was to accomplish this, 'Operation Peace for Galilee', was 'to put all the settlements in Galilee out of the reach of artillery ... positioned in Lebanon'. Behind the modest definition, however, lay the contours of a plan whereby Lebanon might be aided finally to acquire a reasonable government, one even headed perhaps by a friendly-to-Israel President, Bashir Gemayel, the well-connected young commander of the Maronite militia, the Phalange. In this way, it might be possible to secure, and ensure, tranquillity for Israel's north, as well as gain a second non-belligerent Arab neighbour. In the face of subsequently varying, often contradictory reports as to who in Israel's Government knew and approved of this grand design, who disapproved of it, who was adequately informed about it and who kept in ignorance of its intended scope, the best that can be said is that confusion itself tragically characterized almost everything about the only Israeli war regarding which national consensus has not held. In addition to nearly 700 new IDF graves, the controversy over the war left social and political scars which have, in no way, yet healed.

Operation 'Peace for Galilee' was launched on 6 June 1982, the igniting match being the shooting, in London's Park Lane, of Israel's Ambassador to the United Kingdom by hit men of a breakaway PLO group. On the face of it, the campaign, as Prime Minister Begin wrote to President Reagan, was to be a matter of pushing the PLO back 'a distance of forty kilometres to the north', something that would be over and done with in a few days and was therefore endorsed by the Knesset. It did not stop there. The initial objectives were achieved within three days, but the IDF charged on, pulverizing PLO forces, seizing enormous amounts of PLO arms and ammunition, putting out of commission Syrian armour, aircraft and dozens of lethal SAM batteries, and reaching positions around Beirut that, by 14 June, entrapped PLO survivors in an iron embrace. There seemed to be a constant time lag (as well as a notable lack of clarity) in the information reaching Israel about all this, even that given by the Defence Minister to the cabinet. Vitally important decisions were being made, often without prior consultation, and, above all, there was a sharp rise in the number of Israeli casualties.

The 'few days' of fighting lengthened into gruelling combat, much of the gnawing worry at home — and strong condemnation of Israel by the international media — centring on what became the two-month siege of Beirut. The core of terrorist organizations for a decade, Beirut was possibly the most difficult city in the world in which to wage a war, divided as it was

95 General Ariel Sharon, the Israeli Defence Minister who launched 'Operation Peace for Galilee'.

96 Israeli armour patrolling the security zone across the border from Israel, Marjayoun, Lebanon.

between the PLO, rival Moslem and Christian militias, the Lebanese army and the Syrians. It took weeks of artillery duels, street fighting and Israeli air and naval activity against heavy PLO and Syrian resistance before the PLO agreed, on 12 August, to withdraw under Israeli conditions.

No one, including, it can be assumed, the architects of the grand design, had imagined that Stage I would take so long; now Stage II began. On 24 August, Bashir Gemayel was voted in as Lebanon's President; on 14 September, he was assassinated. The consequences of the murder were various: the first thing to happen was the IDF's massive entry into west Beirut; the next, by far the most publicized, most misunderstood event of the war, being the massacre of hundreds of Palestinians in Sabra and Shatilla, two refugee camps in southern Beirut. On 16 September, Phalangist gunmen entered the camps, given permission to carry out 'mopping-up' operations in an Israeli effort to transfer authority to the Lebanese. Next day, when Israeli soldiers ordered the Phalange out, they found some 500 dead men, women and children. The Kahan Commission of Inquiry, formed in Israel in response to local outrage and grief, absolved the Government of 'direct' responsibility, stressed that the possibility of Phalange retaliation for Gemayel's murder could and should have been foreseen, recommended that Defence Minister Sharon (bearing 'personal responsibility') either resign or be dismissed, and stated that it had arrived at 'grave conclusions' regarding the Chief of Staff but was indicating no action – presumably because his appointment was about to expire.

That was in February 1983; the IDF had spent a tough, cold winter in Lebanon, preyed upon by snipers, forever at the mercy of mines, 'bogged down in the Lebanese quagmire', to quote the authors of an early Israeli book on the war. There was no easy way to guarantee the preservation of peace in Galilee; the Lebanese situation was as murky as ever; the new President, Amin Gemayel, who took his slain brother's place, seemed unable to exert significant authority. 'Agonized' was one way of summing up the frame of mind in Israel about a war that had so far exceeded its original limits and the benefits of which were rapidly diminishing. It also described Menachem Begin's dark mood.

The blows had been many: he had made a fatal mistake about the war in Lebanon, assured that it would end rapidly, that it would cost few lives and that it would radically improve Israel's standing in the entire Middle East – none of which had occurred. Late in 1982, he mourned his life's companion Aliza, who died while he was in the US; he was also hampered by a painful hip injury. At seventy, decline and despondence accompanying the chain of irreversible disasters, making a burden he could no longer bear, Begin resigned. In September 1983, he said: 'I cannot go on', and never left his Jerusalem home again, save for the hospital once or twice, seeing only his family and a handful of chosen friends. The fire had gone out, maybe doused by the melting snows of Lebanon.

Baffled, sorrowing, the Likud turned to Yitzhak Shamir. Once an all-powerful member of the pre-state Stern group, later a Herut leader, a former Speaker of the Knesset and Dayan's successor as Israel's Foreign Minister in 1980, Shamir's new job as Israel's seventh Prime Minister was beset by problems. Another winter would pass before the IDF, withdrawing in stages, finally left Lebanon; the return of six Israeli prisoners of war held by the PLO, in exchange for 4,500 Palestinians, Libyans, Saudi Arabians, Iraqis (out of a total of 9,000-odd suspected terrorists captured in 'Operation Peace for Galilee'), had been violently opposed by a sizeable segment of the Israeli public; the activities of a Jewish underground group — made up mostly of Orthodox settlers on the West Bank, eager to take the law into their own hands to end a resurgence of Arab terror within the country — were not only highlighting but also sharpening basic differences of approach within the electorate as to the future of the administered territories; and Israel's inflationary economic situation was becoming dire.

In July 1984, elections were held for the eleventh Knesset; the Labour Alignment won 39.4 per cent of the votes, the Likud 31.9 per cent; some of the thirteen other small parties, splitting the rest of the votes between them, were obvious coalition partners for one or the other of the two big blocs.

A brief explanation is needed of Israel's electoral system, i.e. proportional representation. Israeli parties present complete slates (120 names), listing candidates in the order of party priorities. On election day, the Israeli voter casts a ballot for the one party list of his or her choice, the whole country being a single constituency, as it were, and Knesset seats being assigned to each party in proportion to its percentage of the total national vote. For decades, Israelis have discussed other systems which would permit voters directly to affect election outcome, but nothing has yet been done to this end. It is also important to note that no party has ever obtained a majority in the Knesset and that Israel has always been ruled by coalitions.

In September 1984, to meet the various 'acute' crises facing the nation,

97 Prime Minister Yitzhak Shamir (nearest the camera on left) meets leaders of Israel's Arab community, Jerusalem 1984.

98 Prime Minister Shimon Peres with King Hassan of Morocco, July 1986.

a Government of National Unity was formed. It differed from previous coalitions in that it gave both the Labour Alignment and the Likud, with their respective satellites, a chance to govern – each bloc being granted equal innings of twenty-five months in rotation. The Alignment went first, with Shimon Peres as Prime Minister. This arrangement, remarkable in any society, may be considered even more so in one so disputatious and politicized. None the less, it was contemplated and implemented, and proved, once more, the strength of Israel's flair for unconventional solutions when the going gets rough enough.

Except for ending the war in Lebanon and its economic achievements, the experiment was not a great success, though the uneasy partnership held until the elections to the twelfth Knesset on 1 November 1988.

In many ways, the last years of the Labour movement's reign typified the malaise of regimes that have ruled for too long. Among the presenting symptoms were a series of scandals over corruption made possible by the averted gaze of party stalwarts, an overworked 'old boy' network, and the direct involvement of people holding important government jobs. The exposure of these did more than shock the public; it boosted the stock of those who had fought the well-entrenched highly centralized government-controlled economic system, reinforcing their longing for economic liberalism and the freer, more profitable pursuit of private enterprise – all of which, in 1977, the Likud Government undertook to provide in order, it declared, to restore health to a chronically ailing economy. The new Finance Minister promptly instituted a *laissez-faire* policy, among others easing irksome currency regulations including those pertaining to foreign travel and the amount of foreign currency citizens would be permitted to keep at home or transfer abroad. The Government also reached out to big investors, promising an atmosphere in which the business community, local as well as international, would feel itself a welcome part of an imaginative, creative and permissive thrust, certain to be of benefit all round and to put an end to the canard that the only way to make a small fortune in Israel was to bring a large one with you.

The measures were of benefit, but not quite all round. Private consumption immediately soared; Israel's real economic status declined accordingly; money had to be borrowed wherever possible – which also cost a lot of money and made the national debt per person the heaviest in the world; and – despite the new dispensation – Israelis did not give up a variety of bad fiscal habits, including more than a modicum of income tax evasion.

Prophets of doom predicted the worst, warned of bursting bubbles and of the perils implicit in letting levels of public expectation rise so steeply and quickly. Israel's most generous backer, the US (some $3 billion per annum in various forms of aid), called sternly for belt-tightening in the face of inflation which, by 1983, reached an annual rate of about 800 per cent.

The Government, haunted by fear of creating unemployment, was initially reluctant to cut budgets, although, in the end, even the formerly sacrosanct Defence budget was slashed as were others. The Israeli linkage of salaries not only to the cost-of-living index but also of one sector to another, produces a domino effect in which, for example, if the Government (still the ultimate employer of about three-quarters of the working population) decides to pay higher real wages to the doctors it employs, it follows, as night the day, that nurses will also (and shortly) bid for and receive more money. And so on through most of the white-and-blue collar ranks. One result is that the Government has not been spared its share of strikes, slowdowns and labour disputes. From 1984 on, with the co-operation of the Histadrut, it managed to bring inflation down to the 1988 rate of 17 or 18 per cent.

Two events that accompanied Israel's entry into its fifth decade in the spring of 1988 gave expression – albeit in different ways – to the unique character of Israeli life, to the special nature of the experience shared by much of the population (4,425,000 of which 82 per cent were Jews) and to the nation's continuing uncertainty as to what the future might hold and the realistic chances of peace – if not now, then soon. In Jerusalem, following a fourteen-month-long public trial, John Demanjuk, Ivan the Terrible of Treblinka, was sentenced to death for war crimes, crimes against humanity and crimes against the Jews. The second and possibly the last of such trials to take place in Israel, the hearings served not only the cause of justice, but also to remind young Israelis of what happened only a few years before the founding of the state. For many, the gruelling testimonies of a handful of elderly Holocaust survivors gave added meaning and depth to the fortieth-birthday celebrations.

Dominating everything, however, was the uprising of Arabs which began in December 1987 in the refugee camps of the Israeli-administered Gaza Strip, rapidly spread to the West Bank, touched East Jerusalem and were not over even by the end of 1988, having turned, in the interim, into a major attraction for the international media.

What typified the mob violence was the Arab choice of stoning as the ideal weapon with which to attack patrolling Israeli troops, forbidden to fire

99, 100 'Possibly the greatest success to date are the Israelis themselves.' Above: The Israel Book Week caters to and attracts virtually all ages and most tastes, its wares ranging from translations of international best-sellers to hot-off-the-press Hebrew novels and essays through to popular books and periodicals published by the IDF. Rightt: Standards of excellence prevail also in the application of scientific research to the betterment of life. Here at the solar research facility of the Weizmann Institute of Science, ways are sought to utilize Israel's abundant sunshine and thus contribute to the common good beyond the state's borders.

on 'unarmed' rioters and therefore forced to try to control them with tear-gas, truncheons, shots in the air and plastic bullets. The limited IDF response was predictably inadequate; the wave of Arab fanaticism, frustration and hatred hardly abated; instead, Israel found itself charged with 'brutality' against old women and children, facing the opprobrium not only of foreign statesmen but also of Jewish communities abroad. By the winter of 1988, thousands of Arabs had been arrested, were in jail or detention camps; several PLO ringleaders had been deported; the Arab death toll numbered over 200; and the Israeli military presence was tougher and still heavy in the West Bank and Gaza – although Arab workers from these territories were returning to the jobs in Israel they had left months before. No one could predict when or how the *'intifada'* (as it came to be known from the Arabic for 'shaking off') would come to an end.

Not everything since 1948 or, more accurately, since the start of the Return, has happened in the way the Founding Fathers hoped it would, which may be just as well. As it is, the century of Zionist resettlement has been tumultuous beyond belief, much of it filled with anguish, some of it disappointing; independence, the Ingathering, the defence of democracy, all secured under the most difficult circumstances possible – in addition to siege and war. Possibly the greatest success to date are the Israelis themselves, an identifiable new breed – Hebrew its mother tongue, its bond with the Land the natural tie of native sons and daughters, representing a blend of cultures in which something has gradually taken shape which though created in the proverbial melting-pot, can no longer be defined solely in terms of original ingredients – from those ranks a future leadership, and therefore the Israel of the next century, now rises.

Index

Page references in *italic* type indicate illustrations.

Aaronsohn, Aaron, 31, *38*
Aaronsohn, Sarah, 31
Abdullah, King, of Jordan, 39, 77–9
Abraham, 1–2, *3*
Adenauer, Konrad, 113
Africa, Israeli aid for, 114–17
Agnon, S. Y., 135
Akaba, Gulf of, 92, 103
Alexander the Great, 8–10
Algeria, and Six Day War, 121
Aliyah: First, 24; Second, 24–5; Fifth, 44
Allenby, Field-Marshal Viscount, *33*
Allon, Yigal, 75
Altalena, ss, 149, *150*
Anglo-American Committee (1946), 60–1
Antiochus IV Epiphanes, King, 10
Arab League, 59
Arabia, *see* Saudi Arabia; Yemen
Arabs, Palestinian: nationalism, anti-Jewish feeling, in mandatory period, 40–2, 44–6, 49, 50, 59, 61, 64–6; and War of Independence, 64, 73–9; after War of Independence, 79–81, 90–2, 99–102; after Six Day War, 123, *131*; terrorism, 130, 134, 142–6; numbers, in Israel, 94; uprising (1987) in administered territories, 176–8; *see also* Palestine Liberation Organization
Arlosoroff, Chaim, 149

Asian countries, Israeli aid for, 114–17
Assad, President Hafez, 152
Assyria, 8
Attlee, Clement R., 59–60
Attrition, War of, 123–8

Babylonia, 8
Balfour, Arthur James, later Lord Balfour, 35–7, 42, *43*
Balfour Declaration, 34, 35, *36*, 37, 39
Bank Leumi, 30
Bar-Kochba, 12–14, 98
Bar-Lev Line, 128, 138
Bat-Galim, 102
Beersheba, 76
Begin, Menachem, *63*, 148; Prime Minister, 147–8; and Sadat, Camp David, 151–61, *157*, *160*; and Lebanon War, 170, 172–3; resignation, 172–3; mentioned, 60, 113, 146, 149, *150*
Beirut, 170–2
Ben-Gurion, David, 117–20, *119*; early career, 26, 31, 54, 59, 66; proclamation of Israel's independence, 68–72, *70*; Prime Minister, 76, 77, 88, 102, 103, *105*, 112, 113, 117–20, 149; death, 142
Ben-Yehuda, Eliezer, 25, *27*
Ben-Zvi, Yitzhak, 25, *26*, 31
Bernadotte, Count Folke, 77, *78*

Betar, 148
Bevin, Ernest, 59, 64, 68
Bezalel Academy, Jerusalem, 27
Bible, 1, 4
'Black September', 142
Britain, England, 19, 22–3; World War I, 31–4; Suez War, 103, 104; mentioned, 88; *see also* British mandate *under* Palestine; *also* Balfour Declaration
Bunche, Dr Ralph, 77

Cairo, 15
Camp David agreement, 156–9, *160*
Canaan, 2, 4–7
'capitulations', 18
Carter, President Jimmy, 151–2, 156–9, *160*
Ceausescu, Nicolae, 151
Chamberlain, Neville, 50
Christianity, Christians, 12, 14, 15, 19, 94
Churchill, Sir Winston, 55
Crusades, 15–17, *16*
Cunningham, General Sir Alan, 68, *69*
Cyrus, King, 8

Damascus, 15
Daniel, Brother, 94–5
David, King, 7
Dayan, Moshe, *53, 106, 157*; Chief of Staff, 102, 103; and Lavon Affair, 118–20; Defence Minister, 122, 137, 142; Foreign Minister, 147; and Camp David agreement, 151, 152, 153
Dead Sea, 42
Dead Sea Scrolls, 98, *101*
Deganiah, 24
Deir Yassin, 79
Demanjuk, John, 176
Dome of the Rock, 15, *16*
Dreyfus Affair, 28
Druze, 94, 168

Eastern Europe, Jews in, 19–22
Eban, Abba, 90, *91*, 121
Egypt: Fatimid dynasty, 15; and World War II, 59; and War of Independence, 73, 76, 77; and Suez Canal, Sinai Campaign, 102, 102–8; and Six Day War, 120, 122–3; relations with Israel after Six Day War, 123–8; and Yom Kippur War, 135–42; Sadat's peace initiative, 151–61
Eichmann, Karl Adolf, 112–13, *115*
Eilat, 92, 109
Eitan, Rafael, 168
Elazar, David, 142
England, *see* Britain
Entebbe, rescue of hostages from, 144–6
Eshkol, Levi, 118, 122, 134
Ethiopia, Jewish emigrants from, 164, 165–7, *169*
European Economic Community (Common Market), 135
Exodus, 4
Exodus 1947, 62

Fatimid dynasty, 15
fedayeen, 102
Feisal, Emir, 37, *38*, 39
France, 19, 23, 28, 39, 103, 104
Freier, Recha, 44

Gaza Strip, 99, 108, 129, 151, 159, 176–8
Gemayel, Amin, 172
Gemayel, Bashir, 170, 172
Germany: Jews in, 19, 23; Nazis, Holocaust, 42–4, 52–4, 55–9, 95–8, 112–14, *115*, 176; Israel's relations with, 113–14
Golan Heights, 120, 123, 137, 140, 147, 151
'Good Fence', 168
Greenwald, Malkiel, 96
Guatemala, Israel recognized by, 90

Index

Hadad, Major Saad, 168
Hadassah, 45
Haganah, 42, 46–9, 52, 53, 60–1, 66, 72, 73–6, 149
Haifa, 42, 46, 79
Hannukah, 11
Hashomer, 25, 34, 40–2
Hassan, King, of Morocco, 152, 174
Hebrew (language), 22, 25
Hebrew Language Academy, 25
Hebrew University, Jerusalem, 42, 43
Hebrews, 2–4
Hebron, 18, 40
Hermon, Mount, 137
Herod the Great, 12, 13
Herut Party, 34, 147, 148, 149
Herzl, Dr Theodor, 28–30, 29
Herzog, Chaim, 144
Histadrut, 26, 46
Holocaust, *see under* Germany
Hungary, Nazis in, 96
Hussein, King, of Jordan, 120, 121, 122, 152, 159, 167
Husseini, Haj Amin el-, Grand Mufti of Jerusalem, 44–6, 45, 52

Independence, War of, 64, 73–9, 74
Iraq, 39, 73, 77, 81, 120, 121
Irgun Zvai Leumi (IZL), 34, 60, 63, 79, 148, 149
Islam, *see* Moslems
Israel (biblical kingdom), Israelites, 1–8; twelve Tribes, 4, 7, 7–8; two kingdoms: Judea (*q.v.*) and Israel, 8
Israel (modern state), 1, 93, 164, 167, 176, 178; archaeology, 98–9, 100, 101; economy, 109–12, 110, 130, 135, 136, 175–6; elections: 1949, 86; 1977, 147–8; 1981, 168; 1984, 173; electoral system, 173; frontiers, 61–4, 65, 73, 76–7, 89, 108, 120, 123, 127, 129, 140; Jewish immigration to, 81–6, 82, 83, 84, 85, 93, 109, 133, 134–5, 164–7, 169; Independence proclaimed, 68–72, 70, 71; kibbutzim and moshavim, 24–5; official language, 25; military service in, 135; ethnic minorities in, 94; international recognition of, 88–90; religious affairs, 93–4, 97; 'Second Israel', 143, 149; tourism, 135; joins UN, 91; *see also* Independence, War of; Sinai Campaign; Six Day War; Yom Kippur War
Israel Defence Forces (IDF), 42, 76, 99

Jabotinsky, Vladimir, 31–4, 40, 41, 60, 149
Jacob, 2
Jaffa, 40, 46, 79
Jericho, 5
Jerusalem, 9; early history, 7, 8, 10; Wailing (Western) Wall, 12, 100, 169; Romans and, 12, 14; Persian capture, 14; Dome of the Rock, 15, 16; Moslem and Turkish rule, 15–17, 18; Crusades, 15–17, 16; Bezalel Academy, 27; Allenby's entry into, 33; Arab attack on (1920), 40; Hebrew University, 42, 43; King David Hotel, 61, 62; Old City lost in War of Independence, 75–6; Israeli reoccupation, after Independence, 88; Old City regained in Six Day War, 122, 125; Arab uprising (1987), 176
Jerusalem, Grand Mufti of, *see* Husseini, Haj Amin el-
Jesus, 12
Jew, definitions of a, 93, 94–5
Jewish Agency, 52, 55, 56
Jewish Brigade, 55, 57
Jewish Colonial Trust (later Bank Leumi), 30
Jewish Legion, 31, 32, 34, 53
Jews, Jewish people, 1; early history, *see under* Israel, Palestine; in medieval and early modern Europe, 18–22; emancipation of, in modern Europe, 22–3; importance of the Land, 14;

Jews — *contd*
immigration to the Land, *see under* Palestine *and under* Israel
Jordan: and War of Independence, 73, 77–9; and Six Day War, 120, 121, 122; PLO expelled from, 142, 167; mentioned, 99
Joshua, 4–7
Judea (ancient kingdom), 8, 8–14
Judea and Samaria, *see* West Bank

Kastner, Rudolf, 96–8
Katzir, Professor Ephraim, 134, *157*
Kenya, relations with Israel, 146
kibbutzim, 24
King David Hotel, Jerusalem, 61, *62*
Kiryat Gat, *111*
Kiryat Shmonah, 143–4
Kissinger, Henry, 140
Knesset, 86–8
Kurdistan, Jews from, *83*
Kuwait, 121

Labour Party, British, 59
Labour Party/Alignment, Israeli, 118, 147, 149, 173, 175
Ladino, 22
Latin America, Israeli aid for, 114
Lavon Affair, 118–20
Law of the Return, 88, 93, 95
Lawrence, T. E., 37
League of Nations, 39, 52
Lebanon, 59, 73, 77, 142, 167–73, *171*
Levy, David, 147
Libya, Arab terrorism supported by, 130
Likud, 147, 168, 173, 175
Lithuania, Jews in, *21*
Lod airport, terrorist attack on, 134
Lotz, Wolfgang, *119*

ma'abarot, 84
Ma'aleh Efraim, *162*
Ma'alot, 144
Maccabees, 10, *11*
Maimonides, 19

Mamelukes, 17
Maronites, 168
Masada, 12, *13*, 99
Matityahu, 10, *11*
Meir, Golda, 64, 77–9, *87*, 114, 117; Prime Minister, 130–4, 135–7, 138, *141*, 142, 148, 153
Mohammed, 15, 22
Moses, 2–4, *3*
moshavim, 24–5
Moslems, Islam, 14–17, 18, 22
Mossad, 112
Motza, 40
Moyne, Lord, 59

Nahal, 76
Nahalal, 24
Napoleon Bonaparte, 18
Nasser, Gamal Abdel, 76, 102–3, *105*, 120, 121, 153
Navon, President Yitzhak, 159
Nazism, *see under* Germany
Nebuchadnezzar, 8
Negev, 76, 98
Nehemiah, 8
Nes Ziona, 24
Netanyahu, Lt-Col. Jonathan, 146
New Zionist Organization, 34
Night Squads, 49
Nili, 31
Ninio, Marcelle, *119*
Nixon, President Richard M., 138

Olympic Games, at Munich (1972), 130, *132*
Operation Kadesh, 103–4, *106*
Operation Peace for Galilee, 170–2
Ophira, *see* Sharm el-Sheikh
Ormsby-Gore, Major W., *38*
Orthodoxy, Jewish, 93–4, *97*
Outremer, 15

Pale of Settlement, 19–22
Palestine, 2, 4; Crusades, 15–17; growing European influence in, 18;

Jewish immigration to, before
Independence, 23–4, *26*, 28–30, 37,
39, 44, 46, 50, 56, *58*, 59, 60, *62*, 66;
British mandate, 34, 39–42, 46, 49–
54, 59–68, 73; UN partition plan
(1947), 61–4, *65*; *see also* Israel, Judea
Palestine Liberation Organization (PLO),
130, *132*, 142, 144, 167–72
Palmach, 46, 49, 76
Passover, 4
Peace Now movement, 129
Peel Commission, 50, *51*
Peres, Shimon, 120, *145*, *146*, *174*, 175
Persia, 8, 14
Petach Tikvah, 23–4
Pharisees, 10
Philistines, 4, 7
PLO, *see* Palestine Liberation
Organization
Popular Front for the Liberation of
Palestine, 144
Prophets, 8
Proverbs, 7
Psalms, 7

Rabin, Yitzhak, *106*, 122, 146
Reagan, President Ronald, 168
Rishon Le'zion, 24
Rogers, William, 148
Rome, Romans, 10–14
Rothschild family, 23–4, 35, 88
Russia, Tsarist, Jews in, 23

Sabbath observance, 94
Sabra and Shatilla, 172
Sadat, Anwar, 79, 128, 151–61, *155*, *157*, *160*
Sadducees, 10
Sadeh, Yitzhak, 46–9, *47*
Safed, 18, 40
Saladin, *16*, 17, 19
Samaria, *see* West Bank
Samuel, Sir Herbert, 40
Saudi Arabia, 59, 73
Saul, King, 7

Sde Boker, 118
Shamir, Yitzhak, *157*, 173, *174*
Sharett, Moshe, *57*, *87*, *91*, *105*, 118
Sharm el-Sheikh (Ophira), 104, 108, 161, *163*
Sharon, Ariel, 99, 148, 153, 168, *171*, 172
Shazar, Zalman, *87*
Shcharansky, Anatoly (Natan) and
Avital, 165, *166*
Shechem, *3*
Shomron, General Dan, *145*, 146
shtetl, 22
Sinai Campaign, Suez War, 103–8
Sinai Peninsula, 104, *107*, 108, 120, 147,
151, 152, 156, 158, 159–61
Six Day War, 120–8, *124*, *125*, *126*, *131*, 167
Solomon, King, 7
Solomon's Pillars, *6*
Soviet Union, USSR, 90, 104–8, 120–1; arms and assistance for Middle
East, 102, 128, 153, 168; Jewish
emigrants from, *133*, 134–5, 164–5
Spain, Jews in, 18–19, *20*, 23
Sprinzak, Joseph, *26*, *87*
Stern Gang, 60, *63*, 79
Struma, ss, 52
Suez Canal, 92, 102, 102–3, 104, 122,
123–8, *139*, 158
Syria: and Maccabees, 10; French
mandate, 39; and World War II, 59;
and War of Independence, 73, 77; and
Six Day War, 120–1, 122; and Yom
Kippur War, 135–42; and Lebanon,
168; mentioned, 152
Szenes, Hannah, 56, *57*
Szold, Henrietta, 44, *45*

Taba, 161
Technical Aid Programme, 117
Tel Aviv, 30–1, 42, 46, 88
Tel Hai, 31
Temple, 7, 8, *9*, 12

Ten Commandments, 3, 4
Third World, Israeli aid for, 114–17, *116*
Tiberias, 18, 79
Tiran, Straits of, 102, 108, 121, 122–3
Torah, 4
Toscanini, Arturo, 42
Transjordan, 37, 39
Truman, President Harry S., 59–60, 90
Trumpeldor, Joseph, 31–4, *32*, 40, 49
Turks, Ottoman Empire, 17, 18, 30–1, 34

Uganda, rescue of hostages from, 144–6
UNSCOP, 61–4
United Nations Organization, 60, 61–4; Israel joins, *91*; and War of Independence, 75, 77; and Jerusalem, 88; and Suez War, 102, 104; peace-keeping force, 108, 121; and Yom Kippur War, 137, 140
United States of America, 39, 59–60, 88–90, 104–8, 138, 176; *see also* Carter, President
USSR, *see* Soviet Union

Wailing (Western) Wall, Jerusalem, 12, *100*, *169*
Weizman, Ezer, 147

Weizmann, Dr Chaim, 34, 35–7, *38*, 42, 59, *87*, 88, 90
Weizmann Institute of Science, *177*
West Bank (Judea and Samaria), 77, 120, 122, 129, 147, 151, 156, 159, *162*, 173, 176–8
White Paper (1939), 50–4
Wingate, Charles Orde, *48*, 49
World War I, 30–4
World War II, 52–4, 55–9

Yad Vashem, 114, *115*
Yadin, Professor Yigael, 99, *101*, 142, 147
Yamit, 159–61, *162*
'Yekkes', 44
Yemen, 73; Jews of, 22, 81, *83*
Yesud ha-Ma'alah, 24
Yiddish, 22
Yishuv, 31
Yom Kippur, 135
Yom Kippur War, 135–42, *139*, *141*

Zichron Ya'akov, 31
Zion Mule Corps, 34
Zionism, Zionists, 18, 23, 26, 28–30, 31, 31–4, 35, 37, *38*, 39, 50
Zionist Revisionist Movement, 34